Flinging Monkeys at the Coconuts

A Traveler's Companion
of Quotations

Collected & Edited by

Trevor Cralle

Ten Speed Press
Berkeley, California

ZERMATT
MATTERHORN 4505m SCHWEIZ

Ten Speed Press, P.O. Box 7123, Berkeley, California 94707.
Printed in the United States of America.
Cover and book design by Fifth Street Design

Library of Congress Cataloging-in-Publication Data

Flinging monkeys at the coconuts : a traveler's companion
of quotations / collected & edited by Trevor Cralle.
p. cm   Includes index.
ISBN 0-89815-575-4 : $9.95
1. Travel—Quotations, maxims, etc.   K. Cralle, Trevor,
PN6093. T7F55   1993
910—dc20   93-8992
                                    CIP

1 2 3 4 5 6 7 8 / 99 98 97 96 95 94 93

This book is dedicated with deep love
and affection to my wonderful mother,
Judith Ann Schuyler Cralle,
"Greatest mom on the globe."

He goes.

Walking away

Shoulders swinging

With Confidence

His joyous, patient

Nature

A gift to us

And again

We say goodbye . . .

**Judith Ann Schuyler Cralle "Train Station,"
June 1989**

Table of Contents

Acknowledgments

The idea for this anthology on travel was inspired by letters I received on my travels from my mother, Judith Ann Schuyler Cralle, who often included quotes and poems in them. Thanks, Mom, for everything. Among the many words of wisdom from my fantastic father, R. K. Cralle, "Never eat food x in restaurant y," can easily be applied to traveling. Thanks to my wonderful sister, Heather Stover, most excellent bro-in-law Rick, and their beautiful children, Cassie and Cameron. If I had to guess, I'd say that Heather's favorite travel quote would be, "Roll on you Bears," with her arm slowly circling overhead and pointing south to the Rose Bowl: Grrrrrrrrah!

Mahalo to my wonderful publisher Phil Wood and Ten Speed Press for believing in me once again. Massive thanks are due to my fabulous editor, Veronica Randall, for sharing the vision of my book with tremendous enthusiasm. Thanks to David Hinds, whose positive attitude and uplifting happy smiles always keep my spirits flying high. Thanks also to Brook Barnum and Steve Konrad. Thanks again to my pals Brent Beck and Jerry Meek at Fifth Street Design for the nice visuals. The book you are holding was designed by them.

Continued thanks to my invaluable publishing consultant and literary agent, Lucky Roberts, for his expertise and excellent advice. Lucky, who's been to Faaa, and lived to pronounce it, also came up with the title.

In addition to thanking the inventor of the Post-it–an essential tool for modern day book research–I would like to express my sincere thanks to the best thing that any writer could hope for–a diverse network of friends: • Amy Agigian • LauraMichele Agigian • Kathleen Aldrich • Peter Beall • Mary Ann Brewin • Stoney Burke • Stanley E. Cardinet • Sherry Carlson • George Colendich • Fred Conrad • Tom Dalzell • Karen Delgadillo • Richard Enos • Robert Estes • Rebecca Fish • Michael Fletcher • Michael Friedman • Suzanne Gagnon • Jim Gardner • Kate Haber • Kristina Harvey • Carol Henderson • Holly Herring • Gary Holloway • Jawara • Dan Jenkin • Nate Knight • Laura Larson • Tom Latourette • Sue Matthews • Paul McEntyre • Ellen Nachtigall • Bernard Q. Nietschmann •

Briggs Nisbet • J. T. O'Hara • Doug Powell • Lee Quarnstrom • Roger Rapaport • Ray Riegert • Kirk Steers • Michelle Anne Stevens • Charles Souza • Jeannie Ten Eyck • Jan Thorell • Mark Walsh • Jim Herron Zamora •

Thanks to my friends who responded when they heard I was putting together a book of travel quotes: Cathy Borg, "Oh, you mean like, 'I travel therefore I am.'" Gabrielle Petrosian, "Traveling is romance." Valerie Jones, "Like, 'Where the *#@! is my luggage.'" Janet Fulrath, heard Val's quote and said, "Well, I think a better one is, 'Where the *#@! am I?'" Marty Frum offered this piece of advice for the car traveler, "When you're on the road looking for restaurants and the establishment's name has any of the two following phrases, 'Fine food' or 'Family restaurant',–floor board it away." Terri Dix, "If you've never missed a plane, your spending too much time in airports." Shortly after causing my friend Scott Cameron to crash his bicycle he said to me, "Remember when traveling, there are no such things as bad experiences, only good stories."

Tucked away in the deep inner recesses of the Green Room, Non Travis and I use to chuckle over the line from the Grateful Dead, "I may be goin' to hell in a bucket, babe, but at least I'm enjoyin' the ride." Dave Kinstle often reminds students on trips, "This is not a vacation, it is an educational experience." And then there's Michael Goldston, who once took a giant breath of desert air and said to a group of complaining hungry students, "Food? Who needs food out here, man; you can eat the air!" Brother Anthony James Misner, who once sent a postcard dated May 24th, 1986 from Geneva, Switzerland: "Let us rejoice!! The Pilgrimage has been completed."

Heartfelt thanks to my dear companion, Lee Micheaux, for all your insightful ideas, fresh eyes, incredible patience, endless support, games of backgammon, a cool cat named Buster, and for sharing the love of the planet. You're absolutely right, "Geography is living."

Happy travels everybody!

Trevor Cralle

Note to the Reader

This companion of travel quotations is intended for all travelers whether you're a tourist, armchair dreamer or full-on, hardcore expedition adventurer. It is my hope that this book will enrich your travels, whether you're thinking of taking a trip, en route to your next destination, or just finished a journey and are reflecting back on it. Travel quotes can often trigger a particular moment or intensify the experience of person or place. Pack these bits of travel wisdom into your bag. Sitting in a train or plane, a cafe, at home or by a campfire, pass these quotes around the circle of fellow travelers and enjoy.

Compilations present problems of inclusion and omission. As Nicolas Chamfort once said, "Most anthologists . . . of quotations are like those who eat cherries . . . first picking the best ones and winding up by eating everything." However tempted I was to include all the cherries I had picked, in the end, I was persuaded to go with the quality instead of the quantity. In traveling through the pages of this book, the reader will encounter some old friends as well as many fascinating new ones. Original sources and biographical data are listed when known. Readers with additions, corrections or missing information are encouraged to write.

Have a wonderful trip and happy quoting!

Trevor "Coconut" Cralle,
en route to the tropics . . .

P.S. Like most trips, this book had to end at some point, but the travels will continue, and so will this book, like a work-in-progress forever. Sometime—who knows how far down the road—I hope to be able to publish a revised edition of this book. I'd like to hear about your own travel philosophy. What does travel mean to you?

Trevor Cralle c/o Ten Speed Press, Box 7123, Berkeley, CA 94707

Wanderlust

There is something in October sets the gypsy blood astir.

**Bliss Carman (1861-1929) Canadian poet,
"A Vagabond Song"**

FLINGING MONKEYS AT THE COCONUTS

My favorite thing is to go where I have never been.

Diane Arbus (1923-1971) American photographer, *Diane Arbus: An Aperture Monograph*, 1972, Doon Arbus, ed.

I think that travel comes from some deep urge to see the world, like the urge that brings up a worm in an Irish bog to see the moon when it is full.

Lord Dunsany (1878-1957) English-born Irish dramatist, poet, short-story writer, *Holiday*, March 1951

To shut our eyes is to Travel.

Emily Dickinson (1830-1886) American poet

A traveller's thoughts in the night
Wander in a thousand miles of dreams.

Wang Wei (17th c.) Chinese poet, courtesan, priestess, "Seeking A Mooring"

I hear a locomotive's whistle in the night, far-away places shout their longing and I turn over in my bed and think "Traveling!"

Kurt Tucholsky (1890-1935) German poet

It is very difficult to say where a voyage begins.
First of course there must be a dream,
a longing for out-of-the-way places.

Peter Hamilton (b. 1922) Indian-born English sailor, *The Restless Wind*, 1961

A pilgrimage begins with our first conception of it.

Master Subramuniya

Most of us have dreamed, if just for a moment, of chucking life's encumbrances and wandering free through exotic ports of mystery and magic.

Theodora Nelson and Andrea Gross, American travel consultants, *Good Books for the Curious Traveler: Asia and the South Pacific*, 1989

WANDERLUST

The *romantic*—that was what I wanted. I hungered for the romance of the sea, and foreign ports, and foreign smiles. I wanted to follow the prow of a ship, any ship, and sail away, perhaps to China, perhaps to Spain, perhaps to the South Sea Isles, there to do nothing all day long but lie on a surf-swept beach and fling monkeys at the coconuts.

Richard Halliburton (1900-Lost At Sea 1939) American adventurer, *The Royal Road To Romance*, 1925

ETHIOPIA

Four hoarse blasts of a ship's whistle still raise the hair on my neck and set my feet to tapping. The sound of a jet, an engine warming up, even the clopping of shod hooves on pavement brings on the ancient shudder, the dry mouth and vacant eye, the hot palms and the churn of stomach high up under the rib cage.

John Steinbeck (1902-1968) American novelist, *Travels with Charley*, 1961

Never a ship sails out of the bay
But carries my heart as a stowaway.

Roselle Mercer Montgomery (d. 1933) American poet, "The Stowaway"

EUROPE

I myself have been tempted for a long time by the cloud-moving wind—filled with a strong desire to wander.

Matsuo Basho (1644-1694) Japanese poet, "The Narrow Road to the Deep North"

What child has not traveled by spinning a globe?

Thurston Clarke (b. 1946) American writer, *Equator*, 1988

Now when I was a little chap I had a passion for maps. I would look for hours at South America, or Africa, or Australia, and lose myself in all the glories of exploration. At that time there were many blank spaces on the earth, and when I saw one that looked particularly inviting on a map (but they all look like that) I would put my finger on it and say, "When I grow up I will go there." . . . [Marlow]

Joseph Conrad (1857-1924) Polish-born British novelist, *Heart of Darkness*, 1910

FLINGING MONKEYS AT THE COCONUTS

Terra Incognita: these words stir the imagination.
Through the ages men have been drawn to unknown
regions by Siren voices, echoes of which ring in our ears
today when on modern maps we see spaces labelled
"unexplored," rivers shown by broken lines, islands
marked "existence doubtful . . ."

**John K. Wright (1891-1969) American
geographer, Presidential address to the
Association of American Geographers, 1946**

I found the blank spots on the maps irresistible.

**Eric Hansen (b. 1948) American travel writer,
Stranger in the Forest, 1988**

Maybe I'm a Gypsy. I don't know,
But every time I see an afterglow
Of flaming sun upon a distant rise,
The spell of open trails gets in my eyes.
And when the wind blows in the early dawn
Over the misty mountains I would be gone,
In eagerness, for another field to know,
Another sun and another afterglow.

Anonymous

NEW MEXICO

There is no English word for a type of feeling which the
Japanese call "yugen." To watch the sun sink behind a
flower-clad hill, to wander on and on in a huge forest
without thought of return, to stand upon the shore and
gaze after a boat that disappears behind distant islands,
to contemplate the flight of wild geese seen and lost
among the clouds.

**Alan Watts (1915-1973) English-born American
philosopher, *The Book: On the Taboo Against
Knowing Who You Are,* 1966**

To go away and be a tramp again, free and
unencumbered as I used to be, even if it means all sorts
of new ordeals!

**Isabelle Eberhardt (1877-1904) Swiss traveler,
The Passionate Nomad, 1987**

4

MACHEATH: . . . I would love you all the day,
POLLY: Every night would kiss and play,
MACHEATH: If with me you'd fondly stray
POLLY: Over the hills and far away.

**John Gay (1685–1732) English writer,
"Were I Laid on Greenland's Coast"
The Beggar's Opera, 1728**

While all those tender things
love, friendship, home
That haunt the dreams of all of us
who drift and roam
We trade for worthless stardust
which we vainly seek
In nameless valleys lost behind
some mist enshrouded peak.

**Don Blanding (1894–1957) American poet,
"The Drifter," *Today is Here*, 1946**

All travel is a quest, a conscious or unconscious
searching for something that is lacking in our lives
or ourselves.

**Freya Stark (b. 1893) French-born English travel
writer, photographer**

. . . a good part of all longing to travel consists in a
yearning for people one has never seen, a lust for the
new–to look into strange eyes, strange faces, to rejoice
in unknown human types and manners.

**Thomas Mann (1875–1955) German novelist,
Felix Krull, 1954**

When the virus of restlessness begins to take
possession of a wayward man, and the road away from
Here seems broad and straight and sweet, the victim
must first find in himself a good and sufficient reason
for going. This to the practical bum is not difficult.

**John Steinbeck (1902–1968) American novelist,
Travels with Charley, 1961**

Got to move on, got to travel, walk away my blues.

Terry and Renny Russell, American authors,
***On the Loose,* 1967**

Something hidden. Go and find it.
Go and look behind the Ranges—
Something lost behind the Ranges.
Lost and waiting for you. Go!

Rudyard Kipling (1865-1936) Indian-born British
author, "The Explorer"

The little Road says, Go;
The little House says, Stay;
And oh, it's bonny here at home,
But I must go away.

Josephine Preston Peabody (1874-1922)
American poet, playwright, "The House and the
Road," ***Collected Poems,* 1927**

Passage, immediate passage!
The blood burns in my veins!
. . . Have we not stood here like trees
in the ground long enough?

Walt Whitman (1819-1892) American poet

6

I have traveled widely in my lifetime, having been struck by the virus at an early age and having, as yet, developed no antibodies to harden my resistance or immunity.

Caskie Stinnett (b. 1911) American writer, *Grand and Private Pleasures*, 1977

I do not hold that a traveler must be born with the urge to wander, or even leave home at an early age. But I am convinced that the impulse for wandering comes effortlessly to the young, and one risks losing it if he or she waits too long to act.

Coleman Lollar (b. 1946) American photo-journalist, *Travel & Leisure*, October 1991

Since life is short and the world is wide, the sooner you start exploring it the better. Soon enough the time will come when you are too tired to move farther than the terrace of the best hotel. Go now.

Simon Raven (b. 1927) British novelist, dramatist, "Travel: A Moral Primer," *The Spectator*, August 9, 1968

There is no perfect time to get away . . . just do it!

Anonymous

Leap before you look.

Old Slavonic maxim

Why Travel?

The world is a book, and those who do not travel,
read only a page.

**St. Augustine (354-430) Tagaste-born (Algeria)
Bishop of Hippo, Christian philosopher**

Why Not Stay at Home?

Approve the traveler who never went.

James Reeves (b. 1909) English poet

The soul is no traveler; the wise man stays at home. . . .
Travelling is a fool's paradise.

**Ralph Waldo Emerson (1803–1882) American
essayist, poet, philosopher, "Self-Reliance,"
Essays: First Series, 1841**

One may know the world without going out of doors. . . .
The further one goes, the less one knows.

**Lao-tzu (c. 604–c. 531 B.C.) Chinese
philosopher, *The Way of Lao-tzu***

The wise traveller travels only in imagination . . . Those
are the best journeys that you take at your own fireside,
for then you lose none of your illusions.

**W. Somerset Maugham (1874–1965)
French-born English novelist**

It is not worth while to go around the world to count
the cats in Zanzibar.

**Henry David Thoreau (1817–1862) American
poet, essayist, philosopher**

I should like to spend the whole of my life traveling
abroad, if I could anywhere borrow another life to
spend afterwards at home.

William Hazlitt (1778–1830) English writer

Journey over all the universe in a map, without the
expense and fatigue of traveling, without suffering the
inconveniences of heat, cold, hunger, and thirst.

**Miguel de Cervantes (1547–1616) Spanish
author, *Don Quixote de la Mancha*, 1615**

He would have liked to travel, if he could, stretched out
on a sofa and not stirring, watching landscapes, ruins
and cities pass before him like the screen of a
panorama mechanically unwinding.

**Maxime du Camp (1822–1894) French
archaeologist, qtd. in Amelia Edwards,
A Thousand Miles up the Nile, 1877**

WHY TRAVEL?

Worth seeing? Yes; but not worth going to see.

**Samuel Johnson (1709-1784) English
lexicographer, conversationalist, in reference to
the Giants Causeway, qtd. in James Boswell,** *Life
of Samuel Johnson*, **October 12, 1779**

See one promontory, one mountain, one sea, one river,
and see all.

Socrates (469-399 B.C.) Athenian philosopher

Chi non esce dal suo paese, vive pieno di pregiudizi.
He who never leaves his country is full of prejudices.

Carlo Goldoni (1707-1793) Italian dramatist,
Pamela Nubile, **1757**

Travel is fatal to prejudice, bigotry, and
narrow-mindedness, and many of our people need it
sorely on these accounts. Broad, wholesome,
charitable views of men and things cannot be acquired
by vegetating in one little corner of the earth
all one's lifetime.

Mark Twain (1835-1910) American author,
The Innocents Abroad, **1869**

The knowledge of the world is only to be acquired
in the world, and not in a closet.

**Lord Chesterfield (1694-1773) English
statesman,** *Letters to His Son*, **1774**

Peregrinations charm our senses with such
unspeakable and sweet variety, that some count him
unhappy that never travelled—a kind of prisoner, and
pity his case, that from his cradle to his old age, he
beholds the same still; still, still the same, the same!

Robert Burton (1577-1640) English poet,
The Anatomy of Melancholy, **1621-1651**

It is suicide to be abroad. But what is it to be at home,
Mr. Tyler, what is it to be at home? A lingering
dissolution.

**Samuel Beckett (b. 1906) Irish novelist, poet,
playwright,** *All That Fall*, **1957**

FIJI

AFRICA

11

FLINGING MONKEYS AT THE COCONUTS

Rather see the wonders of the world abroad than,
living dully sluggardized at home, wear out thy youth
with shapeless idleness.

**William Shakespeare (1564-1616) English
dramatist**

My father had a theory that, as the child in the womb
goes through the various stages of the created animal
world, so in early years it continues its progress through
the primitive history of man: and it is therefore most
necessary, he would say, that children should travel, at
the time when in their epitome of history they are
nomads by nature.

**Freya Stark (b. 1893) French-born English travel
writer, photographer**

Most of us abandoned the idea of a life full of adventure
and travel sometime between puberty and our first job.
Our dreams died under the dark weight of
responsibility. Occasionally the old urge surfaces, and
we label it with names that suggest psychological
aberrations: the big chill, a midlife crisis.

**Tim Cahill, American adventurer, author,
Jaguars Ripped My Flesh, 1987**

Most people think they have too many responsibilities
to travel, especially in the way that appeals to their
fantasies. The hungry spouse, children, job, mortgage,
school, army or Mother needs them. This is bullshit, of
course. Most people are simply too afraid to step out of
the rut to do something they would like to do. Honest,
folks: The world doesn't end when you decide to do
what you want to do, it merely begins.

**Ed Buryn (b. 1934) American writer,
photographer, *Vagabonding in Europe and North
Africa,* 1973**

The fool who traveled is better off than the wise man
who stayed home.

Rashi (1040-1105) French Jewish scholar

How much a dunce that has been sent to roam
Excels a dunce that has been kept at home!

**William Cowper (1731-1800) English poet,
*The Progress of Error***

WHY TRAVEL?

To feel at home, stay at home. A foreign country
is not designed to make you comfortable.
It's designed to make its own people comfortable.

Clifton Fadiman (b. 1904) American essayist

Why seek Italy,
Who cannot circumnavigate the sea
Of thoughts and things at home?

**Ralph Waldo Emerson (1803-1882) American
essayist, poet, philosopher, "The Day's Ration"**

Travel makes a wise man better but a fool worse.

Thomas Fuller (1654-1734) English physician

The far horizons do strange things to me
Winds that blow
Carry me a spirit tipped with flame
To and fro.
And though I stay at home, I go the way
Others go.

**Grace Noll Crowell (1877-1969) American poet,
"Blue Distance," *Silver in the Sun*, 1928**

How shall I know, unless I go
To Cairo or Cathay,
Whether or not this blessed spot
Is blest in every way?

**Edna St. Vincent Millay (1892-1950) American
poet, "To the Not Impossible Him,"
Collected Lyrics, 1959**

Nothing ever bridged the gulf between the man who
went and the man who stayed behind.

John le Carré (b. 1931) English novelist

Travelling is the ruin of all happiness! There's no looking
at a building here after seeing Italy. [Mr. Meadows.]

**Fanny Burney (1752–1840) English novelist,
Cecilia, 1782**

13

Reasons to Travel

Why do people travel? To escape their creditors. To find a warmer or cooler clime. To sell Coco-Cola to the Chinese. To find out what is over the seas, over the hills and far away, round the corner, over the garden wall . . .

Eric Newby (b. 1919) English photographer, writer, *A Traveller's Life*, 1982

Why do we travel? Is it to escape our humdrum lives? To rise above every day minutiae? We all need a fresh perspective and a good look at the world around us. It doesn't mean we must go far away, just somewhere we haven't been in a long time, or ever.

June Lyman, American artist, writer, *Don't Take Away My Passport*, 1992

Now travel, and foreign travel more particularly, restores to us in a great degree what we have lost . . . at every step, as we proceed, the slightest circumstance amuses and interests. All is new and strange. We surrender ourselves, and feel once again as children.

Samuel Rogers (1763-1855) English poet, *Italy*

Without the very predictability of home, there could be no sense of the thrill and adventure of abroad.

Mark Cocker (b. 1959) English writer, *Loneliness and Time*, 1992

One of the great things about travel is you find out how many good, kind people there are.

Edith Wharton (1862-1937) American novelist

People travel because it teaches them things they could learn no other way.

Lance Morrow (b. 1939) American writer, "Is the Going Still Good?," *Time*, May 31, 1982

A day of traveling will bring a basketful of learning.

Vietnamese proverb

WHY TRAVEL?

Travel, for those with their eyes and ears open,
is a great university on the go. The classes and lectures
are in the world's museums, galleries, cathedrals,
and great buildings. They are also held in all the deep
forests, alpine meadows, great deserts, and sweeping
shorelines of this planet. Best of all, you are
your own professor.

Lewis N. Clark

Travel is one of the most rewarding forms
of introspection.

**Lawrence Durrell (1912-1990) Indian-born
British novelist, poet, *Bitter Lemons,* 1957**

The wise man travels to discover himself.

**James Russell Lowell (1819-1891)
American poet**

Travel is a creative activity, one that should enhance the
traveler as well as the places and people visited.

**Carl Franz, American travel writer, intro. to Ray
Riegert, *Hidden Hawaii,* 1979**

Part of the fun of adventuring is going places and doing
things people tell you not to. . . . I've always thrived in an
atmosphere of uncertainty. Whenever I take random
chances that come my way, life suddenly gets
interesting. Besides, it's hard to lead a deliberate life . . .

**Tracy Johnston, American writer,
Shooting the Boh, 1992**

I travel a lot; I hate having my life disrupted by routine.

**Caskie Stinnett (b. 1911) American writer,
"The Transcendental Tourist," *Travel & Leisure,*
October 1991**

Globe-trotting destroys ethnocentricity. It encourages
the understanding and appreciation of various cultures.
Travel changes people. It broadens perspectives and
teaches new ways to measure quality of life. Many
travelers toss aside their hometown blinders. Their
prized souvenirs are the strands of different cultures
they decide to knit into their own character.

**Rick Steves (b. 1955) American journalist, travel
writer, *Europe through the Back Door,* 1990**

15

Travel not only stirs the blood . . . it also gives birth to the spirit.

Alexandra David-Neel (1868-1969) French journalist, explorer

Travel . . . is transformational, the strongest human urge, the thing that keeps us and our world vibrant and alive. It is one's duty to travel, to keep moving, to expose oneself to foreign cultures, foreign landscapes, foreign ideas. Any fool with a thought in his head is out traveling every chance he gets.

**Brad Newsham, American travel writer,
All the Right Places, 1990**

Indeed, it seems that travel is one of the few things in this world that is good for you, besides being fun. Hence, I suppose, came the pious line, "travel broadens the mind." After all, most of us lead limited lives. We are too highly departmentalized. John Brown is a banker. Nothing else interests him; at a gathering where pictures are being discussed he has a rotten time and goes home early.

William M. Strong, American writer, *How to Travel Without Being Rich*, 1937

I suppose there is something absurd about the intense happiness I get out of the simplest travel abroad.

Guy Chapman (fl. 1930s) English author, *A Kind of Survivor*

Journeys bring power and love back into you.

Rumi (1207-1273) Persian poet, Sufi mystic, *These Branching Moments*

Because it is there.

George Leigh Mallory (1886-1924) British mountaineer, answer to the question repeatedly asked him on his American lecture tour of 1923, 'Why do you want to climb Mt. Everest?' *The New York Times,* March 18, 1923

MANHATTAN

WHY TRAVEL?

Our friends cannot understand why we make this voyage. They shudder, and moan, and raise their hands. No amount of explanation can make them comprehend that we are moving along the line of least resistance; that it is easier for us to go down to the sea in a small ship than to remain on dry land.

Jack London (1876-1916) American novelist
***The Cruise of the Snark,* 1911**

To me travel is a triple delight: anticipation, performance, and recollection.

Ilka Chase (1905-1978) American writer, actress,
***The Carthaginian Rose,* 1961**

. . . travel will give you a wealth of experience and pleasure which can be drawn on for the rest of your life a wealth, furthermore, which no government can ever take away. If the very worst happens and you are miserable on your travels (unlikely), at least you will have learnt to appreciate your own country. I have never regretted visiting a single country (though three days in Dubai were enough) . . . . And don't let the feeble excuse of work keep you back; remember the Haitian proverb: If work is such a good thing, how come the rich haven't grabbed it all for themselves?

John Hatt (b. 1948) English author, *The Tropical*
***Traveller,* 1982**

Travel teaches toleration.

Benjamin Disraeli (1804-1881) British
statesman, *Contarini Fleming,* 1832

Travel makes one modest, you see what a tiny place you occupy in the world.

Gustave Flaubert (1821-1880) French novelist

A traveler. I love his title. A traveler is to be reverenced as such. His profession is the best symbol of our life. Going from toward: it is the history of every one of us.

Henry David Thoreau (1817-1862) American
poet, essayist, philosopher, *Journal,* July 2, 1851

FLINGING MONKEYS AT THE COCONUTS

The true traveler travels for the pleasure of feeling himself flung through time and space, absorbing fresh life wherever it is to be found . . .

Félix Martí-Ibáñez (d. 1972) Spanish-born American psychiatrist, *Journey Around Myself,* **1966**

Travel is, for me, the most beautiful intoxicant. The words of travel, valise, for example: what couldn't you pack into that? Where couldn't you take it?

William Matthews, *Travel*

Travel is of infinite worth to me. Its value that nontravelers fail to recognize is you never know which of the available images you'll bring home.

Helen Bevington (b. 1906) American poet, essayist, *The World and the Bo Tree,* **1991**

NEWFOUNDLAND

Travel, like dreaming, is a form of emotional satisfaction, and though you may explain the act of dreaming by the cheese eaten at dinner, you cannot explain so easily the particular images which formed the dream.

Graham Greene (1904-1991) British novelist, "Analysis of a Journey," 1935

If you are a traveller, this is very important because if you travel intelligently, you become what you are, you forget your European roots. You become yourself.

Sri Ramana (1879-1950) Indian sage

What's most important in traveling is experiencing the living human aspects of another culture, not just seeing some dusty antiquities. If you aim to learn about the world and learn about yourself, you can only do it through other human *beings.*

Fred Moore, American author, *Fred's Guide to Travel in the Real World,* **1989**

The treasures found in travel, the chance rewards of travel which make it worth while, cannot be accounted beforehand.

H. M. Tomlinson (1873-1958) British novelist

WHY TRAVEL?

The use of travelling is to regulate imagination by reality,
and instead of thinking how things may be,
to see them as they are.

**Samuel Johnson (1709-1784) English
lexicographer, conversationalist, qtd. in James
Boswell, *Life of Samuel Johnson***

. . . travel sharpens the senses. Abroad, one feels, sees,
and hears things in an abnormal way.

**Paul Fussell (b. 1924) American writer,
The Norton Book of Travel, 1987**

Objects which are usually the motives of our travels by
land and by sea are often overlooked and neglected if
they lie under our eye . . . . We put off from time to time
going and seeing what we know we have the
opportunity of seeing when we please.

**Pliny the Younger (c. 61-c. 112 A. D.)
Roman orator, historian**

. . . this is what travel can always do for you,
whether it be travel by air or sea or cinema. You can
take a trip, and if you are lucky you begin to know a
stranger, who in turn helps you see yourself and your
homeland with clearer eyes.

**James D. Houston (b. 1933) American writer,
"Hawaii's Festival of International Cinema," *San
Francisco Examiner*, November 8, 1987**

We see our homeland more clearly when we are away
from it than when we are in it.

**Nawal el Saadawi (b. 1931) Egyptian, essayist,
novelist, playwright, *My Travels Around the
World*, 1991**

"Wait till you leave the place then," said my father.
"That's when you find out you're Australian. Probably be
surprised to find out how Australian you are."

**Sylvia Lawson, Australian writer, "Pasta Moma,"
Home and Away, 1987, Rosemary Creswell ed.**

It took a visit to England for me to understand how the
Australian landscape actually formed the ground of my
consciousness, shaped what I saw, and influenced the
way a scene was organized in my mental imagery.

**Jill Ker Conway (b. 1933) Australian scholar,
The Road from Cooraín, 1989**

19

FLINGING MONKEYS AT THE COCONUTS

The real meaning of travel, like that of a conversation by the fireside, is the discovery of oneself through contact with other people, and its condition is self-commitment in the dialogue.

Paul Tournier (1898-1986) Swiss psychiatrist,
***The Meaning of Persons,* 1957**

What is the purpose, I wonder, of all this restlessness? I sometimes seem to myself to wander around the world merely accumulating material for future nostalgias.

Vikram Seth (b.1952) Indian poet, writer From Heaven Lake; Travels through Sinkiang and Tibet, 1983

One does not travel, any more than one falls in love, to collect material. It is simply part of one's life.

Evelyn Waugh (1903-1966) English novelist,
"A Journey to Brazil in 1932," *Ninety-Two Days,* 1934

To travel is to possess the world.
The traveler possesses the world more completely than those who own vast properties.
Owners become the slaves of what they own.

Burton Holmes (b. 1870) American writer

Travel itself, even the most commonplace, is an implicit quest for anomaly.

Paul Fussell (b. 1924) American professor of English literature, *Abroad,* 1980

Travel breaks you free of habit. . . . The knowledge that you're going to be leaving home heightens the time before you leave.

Mark Rudman (20th-c) American writer,
A Journey to Italy

For my part, I travel not to go anywhere, but to go. I travel for travel's sake. The great affair is to move.

Robert Louis Stevenson (1850-1894) Scottish novelist, poet, "Cheylard and Luc," *Travels with a Donkey,* 1879

Wandering

"Where are you going?"
"To the mountaintop," replied Martin.
"Ah, like ants we wander," the old man remarked.

Eric Hansen (b. 1948) American travel writer,
***Motoring with Mohammed*, 1991**

There is nothing worse for mortals than a wandering life.

Homer (c. 700 B.C.) Greek poet, *The Odyssey*

Not all those who wander are lost.

**J. R. R. Tolkien (1892-1973) South African-born
English novelist**

Wandering re-establishes the original harmony which
once existed between man and the universe.

Anatole France (1844-1924) French novelist

Real travel requires a maximum of unscheduled
wandering, for there is no other way of discovering
surprises and marvels, which, as I see it, is the only
good reason for not staying at home.

**Alan Watts (1915-1973) English-born American
philosopher, *The Book: On the Taboo Against
Knowing Who You Are*, 1966**

A wanderer is man from his birth
He was born in a ship
On the breast of the river of Time.

**Matthew Arnold (1822-1888) English poet,
essayist, "The Future," 1852**

To the wanderer there is no such thing as time.

**Walter Starkie (b. 1894), *Raggle-Taggle:
Adventures with a Fiddle in Hungary and
Roumania***

A good part of our wandering and homelessness is love, eroticism. The romanticism of wandering, at least half of it, is nothing else but a kind of eagerness for adventure. But the other half is another eagerness—an unconscious drive to transfigure and dissolve the erotic. We wanderers are very cunning—we develop those feelings which are impossible to fulfill; and the love which actually should belong to a woman, we lightly scatter among small towns and mountains, lakes and valleys, children by the side of the road, beggars on the bridge, cows in the pasture, birds and butterflies. We separate love from its object, love alone is enough for us, in the same way that, in wandering, we don't look for a goal, we only look for the happiness of wandering, only the wandering.

**Hermann Hesse (1877-1962) German-born
Swiss novelist,*Wandering,* 1920**

. . . wander and wonder are probably the same word.

**Alan Watts (1915-1973) English-born American
philosopher, interview by *Spiritual Community*
two days before his death, 1973**

Useless to ask a wandering man
Advice on the construction of a house.
The work will never come to completion.

Chinese Book of Odes

Self Discovery

The most foreign country is within

Alice Walker (b. 1944) American novelist, poet

Men go abroad to admire the heights of mountains, the mighty billows of the sea, the long courses of rivers, the vast compass of the ocean, and the circular motion of the stars, and yet pass themselves by.

**St. Augustine (354–430) Tagaste-born (Algeria)
Bishop of Hippo, Christian philosopher,
*Confessions***

I only went out for a walk, and finally concluded to stay out till sundown, for going out, I found, was really going in.

**John Muir (1838–1914) Scottish-born American
naturalist, 1913, *John of the Mountains,* 1938**

The farther she traveled into unknown places, unfamiliar places, the more precisely she could find within herself a map showing only the cities of the interior.

**Anaïs Nin (1903–1977) French-American writer,
diarist, *Cities of the Interior,* 1959**

For myself, indeed, I know now that I have traveled so much because travel has enabled me to arrive at new, unknown places within my own clouded self.

**Laurens van der Post (b. 1906) South
African-born British writer**

But if you travel far enough, one day you will recognize yourself coming down the road to meet yourself. And you will say YES.

**Marion Woodman, Canadian Jungian analyst,
Addiction to Perfection, 1982**

MAINLINER *Flight* INFORMATION

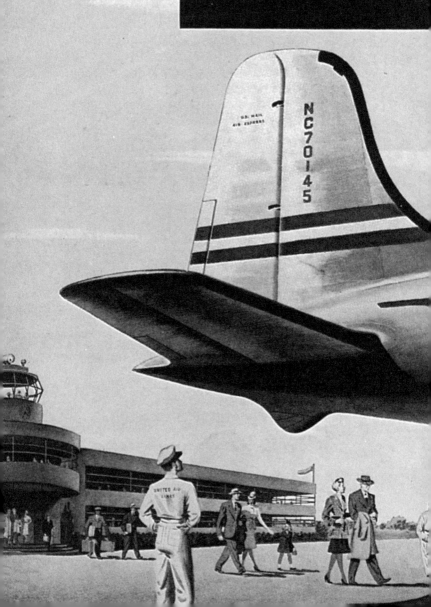

The Traveler

If one must travel, one should do it with the eyes
of a child, the mind of an ecologist, the heart of a pagan,
and the words of a poet.

Kirkpatrick Sale (b.1937) American social critic

Qualities of a Traveler

He that is a traveller must have the backe of an asse to beare all, a tung like the taile of a dog to flatter all, the mouth of a hogge to eat all what is set before him, the eare of a merchant to hear all and say nothing.

Thomas Nashe (1567-1601) English playwright, poet, novelist, *The Unfortunate Traveller*, 1594

If you will be a traveller, have always the eyes of a falcon, the ears of an ass, the face of an ape, the mouth of a hog, the shoulder of a camel, the legs of a stag, and see that you never want two bags very full, that is one of patience and another of money.

John Florio (1553-1625) English translator, *Second Fruites*

Travel like Ghandi, with simple clothes, open eyes and an uncluttered mind.

Rick Steves (b. 1955) American journalist, travel writer, *Europe Through the Back Door*, 1990

Extended travel in countries very different from one's own demands an ongoing suspension of one's personality. There is often no scope or no point, for example, in asserting preferences in matters as basic as food, shelter, and the company one keeps, and it is often even beyond one's powers to direct one's own itinerary. In such circumstances, a sustained attempt to cling to the same habits, the same outlook, the same tastes cultivated at home is to risk being driven slowly mad: it is a truth at least as old as Homer's Odyssey that the resourceful traveler is the one who can adapt to whatever is thrown his way.

Caroline Alexander (b. 1956) American scholar, *One Dry Season: In the Footsteps of Mary Kingsley*, 1989

THE TRAVELER

The traveller must learn to expect discomforts, delays,
disappointments . . . and then, won incidentally or
waiting at the end of the road, there occurs some sight
or meeting or experience that is worth all the effort and,
one knows, achieved only because of it. This is why a
relish for the unexpected, adaptability, and a sense of
humour have regularly been seen as desirable
qualifications for the good traveller.

Kevin Crossley-Holland (b. 1941) English poet,
***The Oxford Book of Travel Verse,* 1986**

If you reject the food, ignore the customs,
fear the religion and avoid the people, you might better
stay at home. You are like a pebble thrown into water;
you become wet on the surface but you are never
part of the water.

James A. Michener (b. 1907) American novelist,
***Holiday,* March 1956**

Those who travel heedlessly from place to place,
observing only their distance from each other, and
attending only to their accommodation at the inn at
night, set out fools, and will certainly return so.

Lord Chesterfield (1694-1773) English
statesman, *Letters,* October 30, 1747

Only the Traveller, impervious to change,
journeys always on.

Jan Morris (b. 1926) Anglo-Welsh travel essayist,
journalist, historian, *Travels,* 1976

The traveller needs restlessness as the sailing ship
needs wind, to waft him from place to place . . .

Phillip Glazebrook (b. 1937) English novelist,
travel writer, *Journey to Kars,* 1984

27

Eye of the Traveler

The real voyage of discovery consists not in seeking new landscapes, but in having new eyes.

**Marcel Proust (1871-1922) French novelist,
"Seascape, with Frieze of Girls,"
Remembrance of Things Past, 1936**

Our destination is never a place but rather a new way of looking at things.

**John Pearson (1613-1686) British scholar,
theologian, "Magic Doors"**

The true wanderer, whose travels are happiness, goes out not to shun, but to seek. Like the painter standing at his easel, he moves constantly to get his perspective right, and feels, though half a country may be spread out to a far horizon in his view, that he is too close to his picture and must get away now and then to look at it with an eye of distance. This necessity keeps him forever on his feet. He touches and retouches the tones of his world as he sees them; and it is to make the proportions more accurate that he travels away from them, to come back with a more seeing and rested eye.

**Freya Stark (b. 1893) French-born English travel
writer, photographer, "Remote Places,"
Traveller's Quest, 1950, M. A. Michael, ed.**

Traveler or Tourist?

The traveller sees what he sees; the tripper sees what he has come to see.

G. K. Chesterton (1874-1936) English novelist

Tourists stay in Hiltons, travellers don't. The traveller wants to see the country at ground level, to breathe it, experience it–live it.

Tony Wheeler (b. 1946) Australia-based English travel writer, *South-East Asia on a Shoestring,* 1985

The tourist who signs up for the round-the-world-in-eight-days jet lag special is left with bleary eyes and blurred memories. Yet the journeyer who immerses himself in a rain forest, clutches the side of a mountain, or punches the spray of a wild river discovers wells with unfathomed depths; windows overlooking infinity.

Richard Bangs (b. 1950) American adventurer, *Paths Less Travelled* [anthology] 1988

Happy nowadays is the tourist, with earth's wonders, new and old, spread invitingly open before him, and a host of able workers as his slaves making everything easy, padding plush about him, grading roads for him, boring tunnels, moving hills out of the way, eager, like the Devil, to show him all the kingdoms of the world and their glory and foolishness, spiritualizing travel for him with lightning and steam, abolishing space and time and almost everything else.

John Muir (1838-1914) Scottish-born American naturalist, "The Grand Cañon of the Colorado," *Century Magazine,* November 1902

. . . travel doesn't broaden, it narrows.
People should stay at home. Whole societies have
been destroyed overnight because of tourists and
bureaucrats.
[Manfred Bird]

Glenda Adams (b. 1940) Australian novelist,
***Dancing on Coral,* 1987**

Would I not, in common with so many tourists, be going
to Tibet to marvel at the Tibetans, not as people, but as
objects in some kind of living museum? . . . and the
expensive hotel, far out of the reach of locals' purses,
reinforce the tourists cosmetic and distanced view of
what he sees as the 'colourful' natives–so long as he
can have his air-conditioning, central heating, bar and
flush lavatory. The victims of tourism are rarely
responsible for the position they find themselves in.

Nick Danziger (b. 1958) English–American artist,
author, *Danziger's Travels,* 1987

Like many English Travellers, I find it difficult to live for
long periods with my own kind.

Wilfred Thesiger (b. 1910) Ethiopian-born English
explorer, photographer, *The Last Nomad,* 1979

We cannot learn to love other tourists–the laws of
nature forbid it . . .

Agnes Repplier (1855-1950) American essayist,
***Compromises,* 1904**

Of all noxious animals, too, the most noxious is a tourist.
And of all tourists the most vulgar, ill-bred, offensive
and loathsome is the British tourist.

Robert Francis Kilvert (1840, 1879) British diarist,
clergyman, *Diary,* April 5, 1870

The traveler was active: he went strenuously in search
of people, of adventure, of experience. The tourist is
passive: he expects interesting things to happen to him.
He goes "sight-seeing."

Daniel J. Boorstin (b. 1919) American historian, *The*
***Image: A Guide to Pseudo-Events in America,* 1961**

THE TRAVELER

It began at first to dawn upon me slowly, and was then
forced upon me in a thunderclap, that I had myself
become one of those uncivil travellers whom I so
heartily condemned . . .

**Robert Louis Stevenson (1850-1894) Scottish
novelist, poet, *The Amateur Emigrant***

The thing you have always suspected about yourself
the minute you become a tourist is true:
A tourist is an ugly human being.

**Jamaica Kincaid (b. 1949) Antiguan writer,
A Small Place, 1988**

Americans are rather like bad Bulgarian wine:
they don't travel well.

Bernard Falk (1882-1960) British author

I don't know where the shame of being a tourist comes
from. . . . When I visit a place and haven't enough time
to get to know it more than superficially, I unashamedly
assume my role as tourist. I like to join those lightning
tours in which the guides explain everything you see
out of the window—"On your right and left, ladies and
gentlemen . . ."—one of the reasons being that then I
know once and for all everything I needn't bother to
see when I go out later to explore the place on my own.

**Gabriel García Márquez (b. 1928) Colombian
writer, "Watching the Rain in Galicia,"
Granta 10, 1984**

In talking with tourists, I learn something not only
about their own country but also about Italy, about
their Italy, which often is quite different from mine.

**William Weaver, American writer, "A Tourist, and
Proud of It," *The New York Times*, March 1, 1992**

Each of those tourists had surprised me in one way or another. It made me think that you never really know anyone until you have traveled 10,000 miles in a train with them. I had sized them up in London, but they were all both better and worse than they had seemed then, and now they were beyond criticism because they had proved themselves to be human.

Paul Theroux (b. 1941) American novelist, travel writer, *Riding the Iron Rooster,* **1988**

Tourist-knocking is easy. It's mainly done by other tourists, the most sincere of whom feel they have an intimacy with the place that the paler arrivistes will never have, a knowledge deeper than a tan. But unless one lives where one is, all of us are tourists.

Derek Walcott (b. 1930) St. Lucian poet, playwright, "A Rediscovery of Islands," *The Sophisticated Traveler: Winter, Love It or Leave It,* **1984, A. M. Rosenthal and Arthur Gelb, eds.**

He did not think of himself as a tourist: he was a traveler. The difference is partly one of time, he would explain. Whereas the tourist generally hurries back home at the end of a few weeks or months, the traveler, belonging no more to one place than to the next, moves slowly, over periods of years, from one part of the earth to another.

Paul Bowles (b. 1910) American novelist, *The Sheltering Sky,* **1949**

Traveling Solo or with a Companion

One of the pleasantest things in the world is going on a journey; but I like to go by myself.

William Hazlitt (1778-1830) English writer, "On Going a Journey," *Table Talk,* **1821-1822**

And enjoyable as it is to share the experience of new and strange sights, no doubt it can dissipate the intensity of the experience of the lone traveller.

Sonia Melchett (b. 1928) Indian-born English writer, *Passionate Quests,* **1992 [anthology]**

When travelling alone, your mind fills up strangely with the people you are fond of, the people you have left behind. It produces odd effects.

Richard Holmes (b. 1945) English journalist, author, *Footsteps,* **1985**

For a moment, I think, my companions too wanted to be alone. As for me, solitude seemed the natural condition of travel. Alone, I was at once more vulnerable and more sensitized . . .

Colin Thubron (b. 1939) British travel writer, "The Old Silk Route," *Granta* **26, 1989**

Travelling alone is not lonely; it's an extremely powerful feeling, very similar to love—it's that kind of strength. It's partly the joy of total aloneness—not loneliness—of being part of the land, as far as you can see and knowing there's nobody you need share it with.

Christina Dodwell (b. 1951) Nigerian-born English travel writer, *Travels with Pegasus,* **1989**

FLINGING MONKEYS AT THE COCONUTS

A degree of loneliness sharpens the perceptions
wonderfully whilst travelling. Alone you note
everything, and note, too, the effect of everything upon
you. You are free to look hard and reflect in peace. The
relationship of two people insulates each in their
relations with the world. A comfort at most times, such
insulation blunts the point of travel.

**Phillip Glazebrook (b. 1937) English novelist,
travel writer, *Journey to Kars*, 1984**

The man who goes alone can start today; but he who
travels with another must wait till that other is ready.

**Henry David Thoreau (1817-1862) American
poet, essayist, philosopher**

He travels the fastest who travels alone.

**Rudyard Kipling (1865–1936) Indian-born British
author, *The Winners (L'Envoi: What is the Moral?)***

When you have no companion, look to your
walking-stick.

Albanian proverb

It is easier to find a traveling companion
than to get rid of one.

**Art Buchwald (b. 1925) American humorist,
journalist, *Vogue,* April 1, 1954**

It is better to travel alone than with a bad companion.

Senegalese proverb

I have found that there ain't no surer way
to find out whether you like people or hate them
than travel with them.

**Mark Twain (1835-1910) American author,
Tom Sawyer Abroad, 1894**

If you want to know a man, travel with him.

English proverb

One travels more usefully when alone, because
he reflects more.

**Thomas Jefferson (1743-1826) American
President, Letter to J. Bannister, Jr., June 19, 1787**

Traveling with anyone is a very ticklish business. . . .
What is your thrill may be my bore. . . . I cannot imagine
what fire and pillage I would commit if anyone were in
a position to keep me looking at things longer than I
wanted to look.

**Cornelia Stratton Parker (b. 1885) American
author, *English Summer*, 1931**

Leave A and B alone in a distant country, and each will
evolve a congenial modus vivendi. Throw them
together, and the comforts of companionship are as
likely as not offset by the strain of reconciling their
divergent methods. A likes to start early and halt for a
siesta; B does not feel the heat and insists on sleeping
late. A instinctively complies with regulations, B
instinctively defies them. A finds it impossible to pass a
temple, B finds it impossible to pass a bar. A is cautious,
B is rash. A is indefatigable, B tires easily. A needs a lot of
food, B very little. . . . The complex structure of their
relationship bulks larger and larger, obtruding itself
between them and the country they are visiting,
blotting it out.

**Peter Fleming (1907-1971) English writer,
One's Company, 1934**

"I learned one thing."
"What?"
"Never to go on trips with anyone you do not love."

**Ernest Hemingway (1899-1961) American
novelist, *A Moveable Feast*, 1964**

For some ill-defined reason, lovers have a particular
penchant for travelling, perhaps in the hope that by
exchanging backdrops for that of the unknown, those
fleeting dreams will be retained a little longer.

Carole Chester (b. 1937) English writer

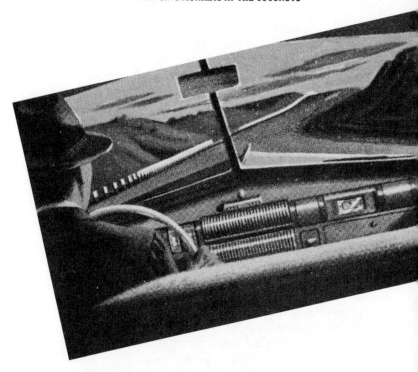

Traveling with another person—friend or lover—is one of
the supreme tests of a relationship.

Charlotte Ford (b. 1941) American writer,
Charlotte Ford's Book of Modern Manners, **1980**

There are only three things which make life worth
living: to be writing a tolerably good book, to be in a
dinner party of six, and to be travelling south with
someone whom your conscience permits you to love.

Cyril Connolly (1903-1974) British writer,
The Unquiet Grave, **1945**

Nothing can match the treasure of common
memories . . .

**Antoine De Saint-Exupéry (1900-1944) French
author, aviator,** *Wind, Sand, and Stars,* **1939**

Traveling in the company of those we love
is home in motion.

Leigh Hunt (1784-1859) English writer,
The Indicator, **1821**

The Educated Traveler

A traveller without knowledge is a bird without wings.

Sa'di (1184-1291) Persian poet, *Gulistan*, 1258

A man should know something of his own country, too, before he goes abroad.

Laurence Sterne (1713-1768) Anglo-Irish novelist, *Tristram Shandy*, 1759

Modern man . . . is educated to understand foreign languages and misunderstand foreigners.

G. K. Chesterton (1874-1936) English novelist, *Autobiography*

In traveling, a man must carry knowledge with him if he would bring home knowledge.

Samuel Johnson (1709 –1784) English lexicographer, conversationalist, qtd. in James Boswell, *Life of Samuel Johnson*, April 17, 1778

Though we travel the world over to find the beautiful, we must carry it with us, or we find it not.

Ralph Waldo Emerson (1803-1882) American essayist, poet, philosopher

Some people travel with a lot of information in their heads before they arrive in a new environment. I prefer to savour first impressions, take them where they will lead me . . .

Carmel Kelly, Australian writer, *The Waters of Vanuatu*, 1985

I can't think of anything that excites a greater sense of childlike wonder than to be in a country where you are ignorant of almost everything.

Bill Bryson, American journalist, *Neither Here Nor There*, 1992

FLINGING MONKEYS AT THE COCONUTS

Never trust anything you read in a travel article. Travel
articles appear in publications that sell large, expensive
advertisements to tourism-related industries, and these
industries do not wish to see articles with headlines
like: URUGUAY: DON'T BOTHER.

Dave Barry (b. 1947) American humorist

Don't confuse your travel agent with God.

Kenneth R. Morgan (b. 1916) American writer,
***Speaking You English?*, 1973**

You don't need a visa for there. There's no problem
getting a visa at the border. It's always nice in the
autumn. You don't have to get there early, it never leaves
on time. I'll be there to meet you. The cyclone season is
over. It's cheaper to take a taxi. All meals are included in
the price. Every room has a view of the sea. The water is
safe to drink. Your taxi will come in a second. Room
service will bring toilet paper immediately. There's no
need to tip. The power failure will be over in a moment.
It will cool down later tonight. The taxi driver will know
where to take you. It doesn't rain much this time of year.
You'll have no problem finding someone who speaks
English. The rain will stop soon.

David Dale, Australian journalist, travel writer,
***The Official Liars' Handbook*, 1986**

To travel is to discover that everyone is wrong about
other countries.

Aldous Huxley (1894-1963) British novelist

THE TRAVELER

The best journeys are those made with the pooled
knowledge of fellow travellers.

**Nick Danziger (b. 1958) English-American artist,
author, *Danziger's Travels*, 1987**

Of all the motives for taking off, perhaps too much has
been made of those lofty goals of mastering a new
language, meeting people, learning about another
culture. Education is doubtless a noble aspiration, but
not enough, in my opinion, has been said about the
advantages of ignorance. Personally I would prefer to go
places where at first I don't speak the language or
know anybody, where I easily lose my direction and
have no delusions that I'm in control. Feeling
disoriented, even frightened, I find myself awake, alive,
in ways I never would at home.

**Michael Mewshaw (b. 1943) American novelist,
columnist, *Playing Away*, 1988**

PAN AMERICAN-GRACE AIRWAYS, INC.
PENNSYLVANIA-CENTRAL AIRLINES CORP.
TRANSCONTINENTAL & WESTERN AIR, INC.
UNITED AIR LINES TRANSPORT CORP.
WESTERN AIR LINES, INC.

Before You Go

He who would travel happily must travel light.

Antoine De Saint-Exupéry (1900-1944) French author, aviator, *Wind, Sand, and Stars,* 1939

Where Are You Going?

It's rather nice to think of oneself as a sailor bending over the map of one's mind and deciding where to go and how to go.

**Katherine Mansfield (1888-1923) New
Zealand-born British writer**

TEXAS

"What place would you advise me to visit now?"
he asked.
"The planet Earth," replied the geographer.
"It has a good reputation."

Ireland

**Antoine De Saint-Exupéry (1900-1944) French
author, aviator, *The Little Prince*, 1943**

I suggested that she take a trip round the world. 'Oh, I know,' returned the lady, yawning with ennui, 'but there's so many other places I want to see first.'

**S. J. Perelman (1904-1979) American humorist,
Westward Ha!, 1948**

"Go West," said Horace Greeley, but my slogan is
"Go Anyplace."

**Richard Bissell (1913-1981) American writer,
playwright, *How Many Miles to Galena?*, 1968**

. . . peculiar travel suggestions are dancing lessons
from God.

**Kurt Vonnegut (b. 1922) American novelist,
Cat's Cradle, 1963**

I haven't been everywhere, but it's on my list.

Susan Sontag (b. 1933) American critic, novelist

For a long time I prided myself I would possess every
possible country.

Italy

**Arthur Rimbaud (1854-1891) French poet,
*Une Saison en Enfer***

That's the place to get to—nowhere. One wants to wander away from the world's somewheres, into our own nowhere.

**D. H. Lawrence (1885-1930) English novelist,
Women in Love, 1920**

All the world was before me and every day was a holiday, so it did not seem important to which of the world's wildernesses I first should wander.

John Muir (1838-1914) Scottish-born American naturalist, *The Yosemite,* 1912

A curious travelers' impulse that I have observed in both myself and in others is that which leads one to seek out places where you have been before, even if nothing very good or even significant happened to you there.

Alice Adams (b. 1926) American novelist, *Mexico: Some Travels and Some Travelers There,* 1990

Why is it that people refuse, or are unwilling, to go back to a place where once they have been happy? If you ask them, they will say that they do not want to spoil a beautiful memory, or that nothing can ever be the same (a wonderful thing can only happen once!).

M. F. K. Fisher (1908-1992) American author, *The Sophisticated Traveler: Great Tours and Detours,* 1985, A. M. Rosenthal and Arthur Gelb, eds.

In any kind of travel there is a good argument for going back and verifying your impressions. Perhaps you were a little hasty in judging the place? Perhaps you saw it in a good month? Something in the weather might have sweetened your disposition? In any case, travel is frequently a matter of seizing a moment. It is personal. Even if I were traveling with you, your trip would not be mine. Our accounts of the journeys would be different.

Paul Theroux (b. 1941) American novelist, travel writer, *Riding the Iron Rooster,* 1988

Traveling Light

She travels grubbiest who travels light.

Erma Bombeck (b. 1927) American humorist

Botswana

Cantabit vacuus coram latrone viator.
Travel light and you can sing in the robber's face.

Juvenal (A.D. c.50-130) Roman satirist, poet

The lineaments of travel. To travel far and often tends to
make us experts in anonymity—but never quite, for we
always carry too much, prepare for too many
eventualities. One bag could have been left behind. We
are too afraid of unknowns to ignore them.

**Alastair Reid (b. 1926) Scottish-born writer, poet,
essayist, "Notes on Being a Foreigner,"
Passwords: Places: Poems, Preoccupations, 1963**

Being mobile, or able to carry everything you've got
is the key to easy foreign travel. If you think you're
strong, try picking up all your equipment and walking
around the block.

**Paul Heussenstamm, American surfer, "Top
Travel Tips" *Surfing,* April/May 1975**

Own only what you can carry with you: know language,
know countries, know people. Let your memory be
your travel bag.

**Alexander Isayevich Solzhenitsyn (b. 1918)
Russian novelist**

Lay out all your clothes and all your money. Then, take
half the clothes and twice the money.

Susan Butler Anderson (20th c.) American writer

BEFORE YOU GO

I never travel without my diary. One should always have
something sensational to read in the train.

**Oscar Wilde (1856–1900) Irish-born British
playwright, poet, short-story writer,
The Importance of Being Earnest, 1899**

I think that to get under the surface and really
appreciate the beauty of any country, one has to go
there poor.

**Grace Moore (1898–1947) American singer,
actress, *You're Only Human Once*, 1944**

Travel Books and Travel Writing

There is no frigate like a book
To take us lands away.

Emily Dickinson (1830–1886) American poet,
***No. 1263*, c. 1873**

Armchair travel—described by Longfellow as "travels by
the fireside . . . while journeying with another's feet"—is
a delightful form of reading as well as invaluable
preparation for a real trip.

Maggy Simony (b. 1920) American author,
***Traveler's Reading Guides*, 1981, vol. 1—Europe**

Books have always been an essential part of travel for
me; wherever I go, my armchair adventures commingle
intimately with actual ones.

Tracy Johnston, American writer,
***Shooting the Boh*, 1992**

The world is a country which nobody ever yet knew by
description; one must travel through it one's self to be
acquainted with it.

Lord Chesterfield (1694–1773) English statesman

Most people who travel look only at what they are
directed to look at. Great is the power of the
guidebook-maker, however ignorant.

John Muir (1838–1914) Scottish-born American
naturalist, in camp at Glacier Bay (1890),
***Travels in Alaska*, 1915**

BEFORE YOU GO

There should be a bit of the author's blood in the ink of a travel book.

Edward Hoagland (b. 1932) American novelist, travel writer, essayist

It is far easier to travel than to write about it.

David Livingstone (1813-1873) Scottish missionary, explorer

Not every writer, of course, who travels is a traveler—no more than is every traveler who writes a writer.

Keath Fraser (b. 1944) Canadian writer, *Bad Trips*, 1991 [anthology]

Travel books I now think are like cookery books and recipes. Lovely bedtime reading but when you've read them you should go your own way.

Jeffrey Bernard, British writer, "Traveller's Tale," *The Spectator,* 4 May, 1985

For every traveller who has any taste of his own, the only useful guide-book will be the one which he himself has written.

Aldous Huxley (1894-1963) British novelist, *Along the Road*, 1925

Every account of a journey celebrates an event that can no longer occur.

John Krich (b. 1951) American writer, *Music in Every Room: Around the World in a Bad Mood*, 1984

47

Photography

A traveller is one who travels many miles to have his picture snapped in front of statues.

Max Gralnick (b. 1929) American writer

The camera is indispensable to the tourist, for with it he can prove to himself and to his neighbors that he has actually been to Crater Lake.

Yi-Fu Tuan (b. 1930) Chinese geographer,
***Topophilia,* 1974**

Coachload of German tourists standing by the bank of the Dutch canal, north of Colombo, photographing Sri Lankan women washing themselves in the water. I wonder if the tourists would welcome Sri Lankan women into their homes to take photos of them having a bath?

Angus Wilson (b. 1913) British writer,
***Sri Lankan Journal,* 1983**

When I walk with a camera I walk from shot to shot, reading the light on a calibrated meter. When I walk without a camera, my own shutter opens, and the moment's light points on my own silver gut. When I see this second way I am above all an unscrupulous observer.

Annie Dillard (b. 1945) American writer,
***Pilgrim at Tinker Creek,* 1974**

Many beautiful sights are impossible to transfer onto film: rather than intrude my camera into an experience for no purpose, I simply enjoy them.

Galen Rowell (b. 1940) American photographer,
mountain climber, essayist, *High and Wild,* 1983

48

Whenever I prepare for a journey, I prepare as though for death. Should I never return, all is in order.

Katherine Mansfield (1888-1923) New Zealand-born British writer, 29 January 1922, *Journal*, 1927

The day on which one starts out is not the time to start one's preparations.

Nigerian proverb

PERU

Il faut être toujours botté et prêt à partir.

One should always have one's boots on and be ready to leave.

Michel de Montaigne (1533-1592) French essayist

SUDAN

Adding people to a picture helps capture the spirit of a place . . .

Bob Krist, American photographer, *Travel & Leisure*, October 1991

Along the Way

A journey of a thousand miles must begin
with a single step.

**Lao-tzu (c. 604-c. 531 B.C.) Chinese
philosopher, *The Way of Lao-tzu***

Departure

There is no moment of delight in any pilgrimage like the beginning of it. . .

Charles Dudley Warner (1829-1900) American author, *Baddeck and That Sort of Thing*, 1874

The journey not the arrival matters.

T. S. Eliot (1888-1965) American-born English poet

Is there anything as horrible as starting on a trip? Once you're off, that's all right, but the last moments are earthquake and convulsion, and the feeling that you are a snail being pulled off your rock.

Anne Morrow Lindbergh (b. 1906) American poet, essayist, *Hour of Gold, Hour of Lead*, 1973

When the true and sincere traveller pulls the front door shut and turns the key in the lock, he casts himself adrift in the world. For the foreseeable future, he'll be a creature of chance and accident. He doesn't know when—or if—he'll be back.

Jonathan Raban (b. 1942) U.S.-based English writer, *For Love & Money*, 1987

Hitch your wagon to a star.

Ralph Waldo Emerson (1803-1882) American essayist, poet, philosopher, "Civilization," *Society and Solitude*, 1875

May the road rise with you and the wind be ever at your back.

Anonymous

A journey of a thousand miles begins with a cash advance.

Bongo Bob, Owen W. Linzmayer, *Totally Rad Mac Programs*, 1992

Afoot and light-hearted I take to the open road,
Healthy, free, the world before me,
The long brown path before me leading wherever I
choose.
Henceforth I ask not good-fortune, I myself am
good-fortune,
Henceforth I whimper no more, postpone no more,
need nothing,
Done with indoor complaints, libraries, querulous
criticisms,
Strong and content I travel the open road.

**Walt Whitman (1819-1892) American poet,
"Song of the Open Road," 1856**

I have lifted my plane from the Nairobi airport for
perhaps a thousand flights and I have never felt her
wheels glide from the earth into the air without
knowing the uncertainty and the exhilaration of
firstborn adventure.

**Beryl Markham (1902-1986) English author,
aviatrix, *West with the Night*, 1942**

. . . I was enjoying a delightful 'holiday feeling,' knowing
this to be the start not of an endurance test but of a
carefree journey 'as the spirit moved us.'

**Dervla Murphy (b. 1931) Irish travel writer,
On a Shoestring to Coorg, 1976**

He woke us at one o'clock in the morning and put us in
the back of the Volkswagen bus and we drove all night.
It was such an adventure! I remember stopping at a gas
station at around four in the morning so that Dad could
fill his thermos with coffee. When you're a kid, just
smelling coffee makes you feel grown-up. Smelling it in
the middle of the night in a car on the highway made
me feel like the ancient mariner.

**Mark Salzman, American writer, martial artist,
"Peopling the Landscape," *They Went: The Art
and Craft of Travel Writing*, 1991,
William Zinsser, ed.**

At last I was ready for the traveler's roulette to begin,
and drove to London airport to catch the Athens flight.

**Gavin Young (b. 1928) English travel writer,
Halfway Around the World, 1981**

FLINGING MONKEYS AT THE COCONUTS

It was drizzling and mysterious at the beginning of our journey. I could see that it was all going to be one big saga of the mist. "Whooee!" yelled Dean. "Here we go!" And he hunched over the wheel and gunned her; he was back in his element, everybody could see that. We were all delighted, we all realized we were leaving confusion and nonsense behind and performing our one and noble function of the time, move. And we moved! We flashed past the mysterious white signs in the night somewhere in New Jersey that say SOUTH (with an arrow) and WEST (with an arrow) and took the south one. New Orleans!

Jack Kerouac (1922-1969) American poet, novelist, _On the Road_, 1957

Ireland

Of the gladdest moments in human life, methinks, is the departure upon a distant journey into unknown lands. Shaking off with one mighty effort the fetters of Habit, the leaden weight of Routine, the cloak of many Cares and the slavery of Home, man feels once more happy. The blood flows with the fast circulation of childhood . . . Afresh dawns the morn of life . . .

Sir Richard Francis Burton (1821-1890) English explorer, Journal entry, December 2, 1856

Cruise

Travel is the act of leaving familiarity behind. Destination is merely a byproduct of the journey.

Eric Hansen (b. 1948) American travel writer, _Stranger in the Forest_, 1988

To travel hopefully is a better thing than to arrive. . .

Robert Louis Stevenson (1850-1894) Scottish novelist, poet, _Virginibus Puerisque_, 1881

It is good to have an end to journey towards; but it is the journey that matters, in the end.

Ursula K. Le Guin (b. 1929) American novelist, _The Left Hand of Darkness_, 1969

All journeys have secret destinations of which the traveler is unaware.

Martin Buber (1878-1965) German philosopher

SCOTLAND!

54

ALONG THE WAY

I think that wherever your journey takes you,
there are new gods waiting there, with divine
patience—and laughter.

Susan Watkins (b. 1945) American writer

I decided to go away into foreign parts, meet what
was strange to me . . . Followed a long vagabondage,
full of research and transformation, with no easy
definitions . . . You feel space growing all around you,
the horizon opens.

**Nietzsche (1844–1900) Prussian-born German
philosopher, "The Wanderer and his Shadow." *All
Too Human: A Book for Free Spirits*, 1908**

Never look down to test the ground before taking your
next step: only he who keeps his eye fixed on the far
horizon will find his right road.

**Dag Hammarskjöld (1905–1961)
Swedish diplomat**

Itinerary

A journey is a person in itself; no two are alike. And all plans, safeguards, policies and coercion are fruitless. We find after years of struggle that we do not take a trip; a trip takes us.

John Steinbeck (1902–1968) American novelist,
Travels with Charley, **1961**

I don't know what to expect, as I have given up trying to figure out in advance what any foreign place is going to be like until I get there.

Richard Bissell (b. 1913) American writer,
playwright

The joy of travel is not nearly so much in getting to where one wants to go as in the unsought surprises which occur on the journey

Alan Watts (1915–1973) English-born American
philosopher, *The Way of Zen*

I think there is a fatality in it—I seldom go to the place I set out for.

Laurence Sterne (1713–1768) Anglo-Irish
novelist, *A Sentimental Journey,* **1768**

Serendipity was my tour guide, assisted by caprice.

Pico Iyer, Indian essayist, *Video Night in*
Kathmandu, **1989**

A good traveler is one who does not know where he is going to, and a perfect traveler does not know where he came from.

Lin Yutang (1895–1976) Chinese writer

Keeping to the main road is easy, but people love to be sidetracked.

Lao-tzu (c. 604–c. 531 B.C.) Chinese philosopher

A traveler who leaves the journey open to the road finds unforeseen things come to shape it.

William Least Heat-Moon (b. 1939) American
writer, *Blue Highways,* **1982**

56

The whole point and beauty of the journey was not
knowing what would happen next . . .

**Ted Simon (b. 1931) German-born English
journalist, *Jupiter's Travels*, 1979**

The wise traveller is he who is perpetually surprised.

**Vita Sackville-West (1892-1962) English author
poet, *Passenger to Teheran*, 1926**

The trip itself would have to tell me where to go.

**Brian Hall, American author,
Stealing from a Deep Place, 1988**

It's good to be out on the road and going one knows
not where.

**John Masefield (1878-1967) British poet,
playwright, journalist, *Tewkesbury Road***

If you don't know where you are going,
any road will get you there.

M. N. Chatterjee (b. 1888) Indian sage

As long as we're traveling toward the unknown, we're
on the right track.

**Rory Nugent, American author, *The Search for the
Pink-Headed Duck*, 1991**

Maybe experience is like a globe–you can't go the
wrong way if you travel far enough.

**William Least Heat-Moon (b. 1939) American
writer, *Blue Highways*, 1982**

The Soul of a journey is liberty, perfect liberty, to think,
feel, do just as one pleases.

**William Hazlitt (1778-1830) English writer. "On
Going a Journey," *Table Talk*, 1821**

It is either distressing or exciting, according to one's
nature, to find that the trail one expects to lead toward
a certain point may carry one into unexpected
directions.

**Carl Sauer (1889-1975) American geographer,
"The Education of a Geographer," 1956**

Your State of Pleasure–
PENNSYLVANIA

FLINGING MONKEYS AT THE COCONUTS

Two roads diverged in a wood, and I
— I took the one less traveled by
And that has made all the difference.

**Robert Frost (1874-1963) American poet, "The
Road Not Taken,"** *Mountain Interval,* **1916**

When you come to a fork in the road–take it.

**Yogi Berra (b. 1925) American baseball coach,
[attrib.]**

Even in a country you know by heart
it's hard to go the same way twice.

**Wendell Berry (b. 1934) American
poet,"Traveling at Home,"** *Collected Poems
1957-1982,* **1985**

There is a peculiar pleasure in riding out into the
unknown. A pleasure which no second journey on the
same trail ever affords.

**Edith Durham (1864-1944) English artist, travel
and political writer,** *High Albania,* **1909**

New York

Columbia

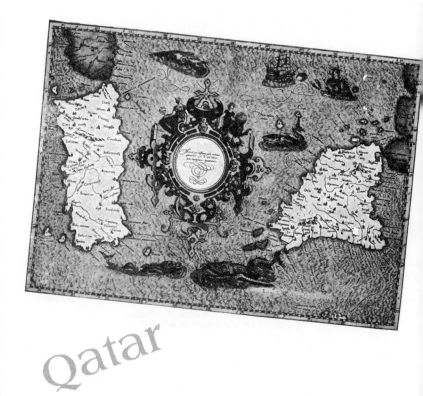

Qatar

Finding Your Way

"*Now I know how Columbus felt . . .*

I'VE DISCOVERED AMERICA !"

. . . there was almost nothing he would have liked
better than to cover the dining-room table with maps
and consider at length possible routings.

**Bill Bryson, American journalist, *The Lost
Continent,* 1989**

The map is not the territory.

**Alfred Korzybski (1879-1950) Polish originator of
General Semantics**

A map says to you, 'Read me carefully, follow me closely,
doubt me not.' It says, 'I am the earth in the palm of
your hand. Without me, you are alone and lost.'

**Beryl Markham (1902-1986) English author,
aviatrix, *West with the Night,* 1942**

Follow the yellow brick road.

The Munchkins, *The Wizard of Oz,* 1939

I could never test it [the warning that Maine natives
deliberately misdirect travelers] because through my
own efforts I am lost most of the time without any help
from anyone.

**John Steinbeck (1902-1968) American novelist,
Travels with Charley, 1961**

FLINGING MONKEYS AT THE COCONUTS

Your bait of falsehood takes this carp of truth;
And thus do we of wisdom and of reach,
With windlasses and with assays of bias,
By indirections find directions out.

**William Shakespeare (1564-1616) English
dramatist, *Hamlet***

So geographers, in Afric maps,
With savage pictures fill their gaps,
And,o'er uninhabitable downs
Place elephants for want of towns.

Anonymous

It is not down in any map; true places never are.

**Herman Melville (1819-1891) American novelist,
Moby Dick, 1851**

Before a journey a map is an impersonal menu;
afterwards, it is intimate as a diary.

**Thurston Clarke (b. 1946) American writer,
Equator, 1988**

En Route

He's made it to Sydney, Australia. And he's trapped there. He can't quite make it to Bali because the two Australian airlines, Ansett and Qantas, are on strike. He won't fly on the Balinese airline, Garuda, because he won't fly on any airline where the pilots believe in reincarnation.

Spalding Gray (b. 1941) American monologuist, writer, actor, *Monster in a Box*, 1991

The terrible claustrophobia of travel began to descend on him. He was trapped in the channels of communication, suffocating in the nothingness of neither-here-nor-there . . .

Michael Frayn (b. 1933) English playwright, novelist, journalist, in transit at Schiphol Airport, Amsterdam, *Towards the End of the Morning*, 1967

A good traveller does not much mind the uninteresting places.

Freya Stark (b. 1893) French-born English travel writer, photographer, *Alexander's Path*, 1956

In travelling I shape myself betimes to idleness
And take fool's pleasure.

George Eliot (1819-1880) British novelist, *The Spanish Gypsy*

On straight stretches of road where the scenery changed slowly, singing often came to the rescue; and when songs ran short, poetry.

Patrick Leigh Fermor (b. 1915) English traveler, travel writer, *A Time of Gifts*, 1978

If travel is to be more than a relaxing break, or a fascinating job, the traveller's interest, enthusiasm and curiosity must be reinforced by an emotional conviction that at present there is only one place worth visiting.

Dervla Murphy (b. 1931) Irish travel writer, *On a Shoestring to Coorg*, 1976

There is something about the momentum of travel that makes you want to just keep moving, to never stop.

Bill Bryson, American journalist,
Neither Here Nor There, **1992**

I wanted to keep going forever, to never stop, that morning when the the truck picked me up at five a.m. It was like a drug in me. As a traveler I can achieve a kind of high, a somewhat altered state of consciousness. I think it must be what athletes feel. I am transported out of myself, into another dimension in time and space. While the journey is on buses and across land, I begin another journey inside my head, a journey of memory and sensation, of past merging with present, of time growing insignificant.

Mary Morris (b. 1947) American novelist,
short-story writer, *Nothing to Declare,* **1988**

I had grown into my clothes the way travellers do who haven't looked in a mirror for weeks.

Colin Thubron (b. 1939) British travel writer,
"Night in Vietnam," *Granta* **10, 1984**

Laundry is the curse of the long distance traveller.

David Dale, Australian journalist, travel writer,
The Obsessive Traveller, **1991**

Hot showers first time in a month.

Mark Jenkins, American writer, *Off the Map:*
Bicycling Across Siberia, **1992**

From whatever place I write you will expect that part of my 'Travels' will consist of excursions in my own mind.

Samuel Taylor Coleridge (1772-1834) English
poet, Satyrane's Letters, ii. [The Friend, 7 Dec.
1809 No. 16. Biographia Literaria]

I never send postcards home from my travels . . .. The writer is obviously gloating: "Wish you were here" means "Don't you wish you were?" A card I received from the Gobi Desert contained the one word, "interesting."

Helen Bevington (b. 1906) American poet,
essayist, *The World and the Bo Tree,* **1991**

On a summer vacation trip Benchley arrived in Venice
and immediately wired a friend:
'STREETS FLOODED. PLEASE ADVISE.'

IDAHO

**Robert Benchley (1899-1945) American humorist,
qtd. in R. E. Drennan, *Algonquin Wits,* 1968**

The pleasure of receiving mail is increased several fold
if, instead of simply devouring it, instantly, at the post
office, you transport it carefully to somewhere
comfortable and relatively private–a pleasant café, for
instance–and savour its sweetness over a cup of coffee
or a glass of beer.

**Ian Hibell, British touring cyclist, and Clinton
Trowbridge, British travel writer,
Into the Remote Places, 1984**

Hawaii

The woods are lovely, dark and deep,
But I have promises to keep,
And miles to go before I sleep,
And miles to go before I sleep . . .

**Robert Frost (1874- 1963) American poet,
"Stopping by Woods on a Snowy Evening"**

On my travels I have discovered that I am usually
making two simultaneous journeys. One is outside
myself, as my eyes search landscapes through train,
plane, or car windows, and I perhaps chat with other
passengers. The other is inside myself, where dreams
collide with facts, loneliness with an urge to seek
relationships, and the question of my real identity
overpoweringly asserts itself.

**Malcolm Boyd (b. 1923) American author, social
commentator**

I was walking through Vietnam's past with the same
ignorance as I had walked through its present. Why
hadn't I read anything before coming? I had entertained
ideas about encountering Vietnam free from prejudice; I
would be a clean slate for the country to write upon.

**Colin Thubron (b. 1939) British travel writer,
"Night in Vietnam," *Granta* 10, 1984**

A WORLD IN ITSELF!

New Zealand

It is delightful to read on the spot the impressions and opinions of tourists who visited a hundred years ago, in the vehicles and with the aesthetic prejudices of the period, the place which you are visiting now. The voyage ceases to be a mere tour through space; you travel through time and thought as well.

Aldous Huxley (1894–1963) British novelist,
***Along the Road,* 1925**

C'est quasi le même de converser avec ceux des autres siècles que de voyager.

Travelling is almost like talking with men of other centuries.

René Descartes (1596–1650) French philosopher, *Discourse on Method*, 1637

For each of us, in our separate ways, the journey involved the redefinition of our relationship to the past and reconfiguring our sense of geography. Just as we know ourselves in relation to others, so I knew how beautiful Australia was only after encountering the real rather than the imagined landscape of England and Europe.

Jill Ker Conway (b. 1933) Australian scholar,
***The Road from Coorain*, 1989**

It is very surprising to discover the importance which politics assume the moment one begins to travel.

Evelyn Waugh (1903–1966) English novelist,
***Remote People*, 1931**

Un viaggiatore prudente non disprezza mai il suo paese.

A wise traveler never despises his own country.

Carlo Goldoni (1707–1793) Italian dramatist,
***Pamela Nubile*, 1757**

. . . actual journeys aren't like stories at all. At the time, they seem to be mere strings of haps and mishaps, without point or pattern. You get stuck. You meet someone you like. You get a rude going-over in a bar. You get lost. You get lonely. You get interested in architecture. You get diarrhoea. You get invited to a party. You get frightened. A stretch of country takes you by surprise. You get homesick. You are, by rapid turns, engrossed, bored, alert, dull, happy, miserable, well and ill. Every day tends to seem out of connection with every other day, until living from moment to moment turns into a habit and travelling itself into a form of ordinary life. You can't remember when it wasn't like this. There is a great deal of liberating pleasure to be had from being abroad in the world, continuously on the move, like one of Baudelaire's lost balloons, but a journey, at least as long as it is actually taking place, is the exact opposite of a story. It is a shapeless, unsifted, endlessly shifting accumulation of experience.

Jonathan Raban (b. 1942) U.S.-based English writer, *For Love & Money,* **1987**

Most of the beauties of travel are due to the strange hours we keep to see them.

William Carlos Williams (1883-1963) American poet, "January Morning," *Selected Poems,* **1949**

The true delight of travel, the one that is going to print itself unaccountably and indelibly on you, seems to prefer to come as a thief in the night, and not at the hours you specially fix for its entertainment.

C. E. Montague, *The Right Place*

On journeys it has happened many times before that something I especially desire withholds itself. Travel is like knowledge: much remains unknown and imperfectly seen, a situation not always remedied by checking museum hours, which are, in any case, changeable.

Emily Hiestand (b. 1947) American poet, writer, artist, *The Very Rich Hours,* **1992**

Arrival

One's first day in a new country is largely a sensory experience: body-contact between the stranger and a myriad unfamiliar sights, sounds and smells. These have an acute—oddly animal—importance while the traveller's mind is uncluttered by personal knowledge or acquired opinions. There is nothing to puzzle over, analyse, dissect; one is merely a passive, though excited, receiver of impressions. Also one's psychic pores are open wide, absorbing messages—their significance not yet understood—from a whole new cultural-spiritual environment. That first day rarely deceives.

Dervla Murphy (b. 1931) Irish travel writer,
***Cameroon with Egbert,* 1990**

The American arrives in Paris with a few French phrases he has culled from a conversational guide or picked up from a friend who owns a beret.

Fred Allen (1894-1957) American comedian,
intro. to Art Buchwald, *Paris after Dark,* 1954

There is no denying that most of us, when we arrive at a place, immediately begin to think of other places to which we may go from it.

Argentina

Robert Lynd (1879-1949) Anglo-Irish essayist, journalist, *The Blue Lion*, 1923

Arriving in a strange city in the middle of the night, standing quite still in the dark listening to the sounds.

Jan Myrdal (b. 1927) Swedish essayist, novelist, playwright, *The Silk Road*, 1979

Was there some fear of travel, in spite of my longing for the day, and in spite of my genuine excitement?

V. S. Naipaul (b. 1931) Trinidadian novelist, *The Enigma of Arrival*, 1987

To awaken quite alone in a strange town is one of the pleasant sensations in the world. You are surrounded by adventure. You have no idea of what is in store for you, but you will, if you are wise and know the art of travel, let yourself go on the stream of the unknown and accept whatever comes in the spirit in which the gods may offer it.

MALTA

Freya Stark (b. 1893) French-born English travel writer, photographer, *Baghdad Sketches*, 1929

67

People

I was once asked if I'd like to meet the president of a certain country. I said, "No. But I'd love to meet some sheepherders." The sheepherders, farmers and taxi drivers are often the most fascinating people.

James A. Michener (b. 1907) American novelist

A journey is best measured in friends rather than miles.

Tim Cahill, American adventurer, author,
***Road Fever,* 1991**

. . . a conversation with a foreigner whom you will probably never see again triggers no signal for caution.

Vikram Seth (b. 1952) Indian poet, writer,
***From Heaven Lake; Travels through Sinkiang and Tibet,* 1983**

On a long train journey we ought, therefore, to present ourselves to the other people in our coach as a wide-open, indestructible vessel into which the acids of truth can safely be poured. We should become for the time like psychoanalysts, making those sitting opposite feel that nothing they can say will shock us or provoke scorn. Travelers are often advised to take a long book on their journeys, but who would devote his attention to a book which will always be at hand when he can turn the dog-eared pages of a total stranger whom he may never meet again?

Quentin Crisp (b. 1908) British entertainer,
author, "Riding with a Stiff Upper Lip," *The New*
***York Times,* 1983**

68

It was my purpose to spy out the land in a very private
way, and complete my visit without making any
acquaintances.

**Mark Twain (1835-1910) American author,
"The Scenery," 1872**

I'm traveling incognito.

Nasrudin, *Sufi Tales*

The quieter you travel, the farther you'll get.

Russian proverb

I experienced that feeling of isolation which is one of the
pleasures of solitary travel: awareness that no one in the
whole world knows where you are, save you yourself,
and delight in the sufficiency of that awareness. *Here am
I alone in the midst of this strange scene.*

**Phillip Glazebrook (b. 1937) English novelist,
travel writer, *Journey to Kars*, 1984**

Some travelers think they want to go to foreign places
but are dismayed when the places turn out actually to
be foreign.

**Margaret Atwood (b. 1935) Canadian poet, novelist,
The Sophisticated Traveler: Winter, Love It or Leave It,
1984, A. M. Rosenthal and Arthur Gelb, eds.**

In foreign places you have to do foreign things.
Everything is experience.

**Jane Graham, Australian writer,
"Two Tales of a Trip," *Home and Away*, 1987,
Rosemary Creswell, ed.,**

It seemed that the deeper I travelled into the wilds, the greater was the people's honour and integrity. Also it occurred to me that perhaps their "primitive" moral values were more civilised than in so-called "civilisation."

Christina Dodwell (b. 1951) Nigerian-born
English travel writer, *In Papua New Guinea*, 1983

Each time I go to a place I have not seen before I hope it will be as different as possible from the places I already know. . . . I assume it is natural for a traveler to seek diversity, and that it is the human element which makes him most aware of difference. If people and their manner of living were alike everywhere, there would not be much point in moving from one place to another.

Paul Bowles (b. 1910) American novelist,
***Their Heads Are Green and Their Hands Are Blue*, 1957**

There are those who never experience travel itself as exhilaration bubbling through the body. They do not tingle when they approach the mountains. They move from place to place while carrying out their duty to report facts and figures back home despite homesickness, dysentery, blisters, bad plumbing, and hard beds.

Jan Myrdal (b. 1927) Swedish essayist, novelist,
playwright, *The Silk Road*, 1979

Their concern was how to pretend they had never left home. What hotels in Madrid boasted king-sized Beauty-rest mattresses? What restaurants in Tokyo offered Sweet 'n' Low? Did Amsterdam have a McDonald's? Did Mexico City have a Taco Bell? Did any place in Rome serve Chef Boyardee ravioli?

Anne Tyler (b. 1941) American novelist,
***The Accidental Tourist*, 1985**

You fly off to a strange land, eagerly abandoning all the comforts of home, and then expend vast quantities of time and money in a largely futile effort to recapture the comforts that you wouldn't have lost if you hadn't left home in the first place.

Bill Bryson, American journalist,
***Neither Here Nor There*, 1992**

ALONG THE WAY

I dislike feeling at home when I am abroad.

George Bernard Shaw (1856–1950)
Irish dramatist

People travel to faraway places to watch, in fascination,
the kind of people they ignore at home.

Dagobert D. Runes (1902–1982) American writer

Wherever you go, you will receive impressions of the
places you see and the people you meet. Do not forget
that those people will receive impressions of you.

Broughton Waddy (b. 1911) Australian-born
British doctor, and Ralph Townley (b. 1923) British
diplomat, *A Word or Two Before You Go*, 1980

There is nothing so strange in a strange land than those
who visit it.

Dennis O'Rourke, Australian ethnographic
filmmaker, *Cannibal Tours*, 1987

When you travel, you are essentially the guest
in a foreign country. You are the one with the
curious customs.

Charlotte Ford (b. 1941) American writer,
***Charlotte Ford's Book of Modern Manners*, 1980**

71

Food

Homesickness starts with food.

**Che Guevara (1928-1967) Argentine-born
Marxist revolutionary leader**

To eat well in England you should have breakfast three
times a day.

**W. Somerset Maugham (1874-1965)
French-born English novelist**

Everything in France is a pretext for a good dinner.

**Jean Anouilh (1910-1987) French playwright,
Cecile, 1949**

Never eat Chinese food in Oklahoma.

Bryan Miller (20th c.) American food critic

I tend not to bother with restaurants that get three
stars in the Michelin guides because they are likely to
be excessively French, while those with lower ratings
have a chance of being Italian.

**David Dale, Australian journalist, travel writer,
The Obsessive Traveller, 1991**

When travelling I make a sincere effort to throw
overboard all prejudices concerning food.

**Norman Lewis (b. 1903) English novelist,
journalist, travel writer**

Never journey without something to eat in your pocket.
If only to throw to dogs when attacked by them.

E. S. Bates (1879-1939) American writer

A traveller's most interesting meals
tend to happen by surprise.

**David Dale, Australian journalist, travel writer,
The Obsessive Traveller, 1991**

If you cannot understand a people's language, you have
only to look at what they eat to learn a great deal—not
just about their food and way of life, but also about
their culture.

Reinhart Wolf, *Japan: The Beauty of Food*, 1987

72

Hotels and Camping

My rucksack was buckling my shoulders forwards instead of bracing them back. I wanted to sleep somewhere: anywhere.

Colin Thubron (b. 1939) British travel writer, "Night in Vietnam," *Granta* 10, 1984

There are few beds more comfortable than a dry ditch in England in June.

Frank Tatchell (fl. 1920s) English clergyman, *The Happy Traveller: A Book for Poor Men*, 1923

You wake up in the morning—be it in some cheap hotel or in a sleeping-bag beneath a tree in a field . . . and the only thing you know for sure is that you don't know where you're going to be that night. That's a strange feeling the first time it dawns on you.

Ken Welsh, *Hitch-hikers's Guide to Europe*, 1971

Guests at the Hilton Hotel are frequently reduced to dialing room service to find out which country they are in.

John Wells, British writer, "Plus ça Change," *The Spectator*, September 15, 1967

In America camping is considered a healthy sport for Boy Scouts but a crime for mature men who have made it their vocation.

Jack Kerouac (1922–1969) American poet, novelist, *Lonesome Traveler*, 1960

An inquisitive young man could pick up a lot of philosophy around a caravan campfire.

Tom Robbins (b. 1936) American novelist *Another Roadside Attraction*, 1971

If you think you are too small to be effective, you have never been in bed with a mosquito.

Bette Reese (20th c.) American writer

I'd rather wake up in the middle of nowhere than in any city on earth.

Steve McQueen (1930-1980) American actor

Cities

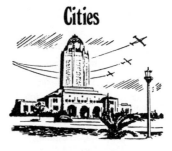

No city should be too large for a man to walk out of
in a morning.

Cyril Connolly (1903-1974) British writer,
***The Unquiet Grave*, 1945**

There are only two rules. One is E. M. Forster's guide to
Alexandria; the best way to know Alexandria is to
wander aimlessly. The second is from the Psalms; grin
like a dog and run about through the city.

Jan Morris (b. 1926) Anglo-Welsh travel essayist,
journalist, historian, *Destinations*, 1980

Cities, like cats, will reveal themselves at night.

Rupert Brooke (1887-1915) English poet,
***Letters from America*, 1916**

The very name London has tonnage in it.

V. S. Prichett, *London Perceived*

If Paris didn't exist we would have to invent it.

***Let's Go Europe*, 1987**

Paris is a veritable ocean. Take as many soundings in it
as you will, you will never know its depth.

Honoré de Balzac (1790-1850) French novelist

If you are lucky enough to have lived in Paris as a young
man, then wherever you go for the rest of your life, it
stays with you, for Paris is a moveable feast.

Ernest Hemingway (1899-1961) American
novelist, *A Moveable Feast*, 1964

74

MIAMI

★ WASHINGTON, D.C. ★

In the city, time becomes visible.

Lewis Mumford (b. 1895) American writer

New York is a catastrophe
—but a magnificent catastrophe.

Le Corbusier (1887-1965) French architect

No city seems to me altogether complete without the
dimension of the sea.

**Jan Morris (b. 1926) Anglo-Welsh travel essayist,
journalist, historian, "Jan Morris Basks in the City
Lights," *Travel & Leisure,* October 1991**

Venice is like eating an entire box of chocolate liqueurs
at one go.

**Truman Capote (1924-1984) American novelist,
qtd. in *The Observer,* November 26, 1961**

IN SYDNEY-IT'S "THE AUSTRALIA"

The Finest Hotel
South of the Line.
Tasteful, brilliant,
distinctive. Enjoys
a world-wide cli-
entele. Delightful
cuisine & service.
Telegraphic Address:
'Austraotel, Sydney'

The Australia Hotel
SYDNEY, AUSTRALIA.

Museums

So you went to the Louvre:
What did you see?

Terry and Renny Russell, American authors,
***On the Loose,* 1967**

How fortunate we are that the British Museum and the
National Gallery are full of objects that are neither
British nor National.

E.R.Chamberlain (b. 1926),
***Loot: The Heritage of Plunder,* 1983**

When I go to Japan, I duly visit the temples and the
museums, but my real passion is reserved for the
always-imaginative stationery section of the great
department stores. And I have Italian friends who,
arriving in New York, head at once—no, not for MOMA
or the Met—but for 47th Street Photo, as famous in
Europe as any art gallery.

**William Weaver, American writer, "A Tourist, and
Proud of It,"** ***The New York Times,*** **March 1, 1992**

I love to wander around in a good store
—it knocks the spots off a museum.

Richard Bissell (b. 1913) American playwright

Sense of Place

Every perfect traveler always creates the country
where he travels.

Nikos Kazantzakis (1883-1957) Greek novelist

Through my travelling experience I have found that first
impressions are the most important ones,
the most truthful.

**Nawal el Saadawi (b. 1931) Egyptian, essayist, novelist,
playwright, *My Travels Around the World*,1991**

The appreciation of landscape is more personal and
longer lasting when it is mixed with the memory of
human incidents.

**Yi-Fu Tuan (b. 1930) Chinese geograpgher,
Topophilia, 1974**

El Paso

For me, a sense of place is nothing more than a sense of
people. Whether a landscape is bleak or beautiful, it
doesn't mean anything to me until a person walks into
it, and then what interests me is how the person
behaves in that place.

**Mark Salzman, American writer, martial artist,
"Peopling the Landscape", *They Went: The Art and
Craft of Travel Writing*, 1991, William Zinsser, ed.**

I doubt Whether I ever read any description of scenery
which gave me an idea of the place described.

**Anthony Trollope (1815-1882) English novelist,
Australia and New Zealand, 1873**

Scenic State of TENNESSEE

FLINGING MONKEYS AT THE COCONUTS

To know a foreign country at all you must not only have lived in it and in your own, but also in at least one other.

**W. Somerset Maugham (1874-1965)
French-born English novelist**

To drink in the spirit of a place you should be not only alone but not hurried.

**George Santayana (1863-1952) American
philosopher, *The Letters of George Santayana*, 1955**

Of course it wasn't really a wild spot. No doubt it is easy to reach the site in a coach from a cruise ship, and walk around it, and motor away before night falls. But a place is as remote as it feels to you, and it is the means by which you reach it which gives you a sense of remoteness.

**Phillip Glazebrook (b. 1937) English novelist,
travel writer, *Journey to Kars*, 1984**

A man who has not been in Italy, is always conscious of an inferiority, from his not having seen what it is expected a man should see. The grand object of travelling is to see the shores of the Mediterranean

**Samuel Johnson (1709-1784) English
lexicographer, conversationalist, qtd. in James
Boswell, *Life of Samuel Johnson*, April 11, 1776**

Surely to have seen Athens gives a man what Swift calls Invisible Precedence over his fellows.

Sir Edward Marsh (1872-1953) English writer

If you ever go to New Mexico, it will itch you for the rest of your life.

Georgia O'Keeffe (1887-1986) American artist

Switzerland is my favorite place now, because it's so—nothing. There's absolutely nothing to do.

**Andy Warhol (1927-1987) American pop artist,
filmmaker**

What does this journey seem like to those who aren't British as they head towards the land of embarrassment and breakfast?

**Julian Barnes (b. 1931) British writer,
Flaubert's Parrot, 1984**

There are, really, only two kinds of travelers:
those who visit the Eiffel Tower and love it,
and those who find it boring.

Leonard S. Bernstein, American writer, poet,
Never Make a Reservation in Your Own Name,1981

But the traveler is a slave to his senses; his grasp of a
fact can only be complete when reinforced by sensory
evidence; he can know the world, in fact, only when he
sees, hears, and smells it.

Robert Byron (1905-1941) English travel writer,
First Russia, Then Tibet, **1933**

Certain places have an aroma that becomes an integral
part of their profile . . . . You can often tell where in the
world you are simply by breathing.

George J. Demko (b. 1933) American
geographer, ***Why in the World: Adventures in***
Geography,1992

. . . The first condition of understanding a foreign
country is to smell it . . .

T. S. Eliot (1888-1965) American-born English
poet, "Rudyard Kipling"

Transience is not the only perspective from which to
view oneself or another country.

Rosemary Creswell (b. 1941) Australian literary
agent, ***Home and Away,*** **1987 [anthology]**

Most of my treasured memories of travel are
recollections of sitting.

Robert Thomas Allen (b. 1911) Canadian
humorist, ***How to Survive the Age of Travel,*** **1974**

When you sit in a spot, your energy
becomes saturated with the tone of the place.
Imagine a teabag that had no flavor, color, or properties
of its own, but only absorbed the qualities around it.
Let yourself sit until you are done.

Fredric Lehrman, American poet, "Steeping,"
The Sacred Landscape, **1988**

There is a rare emotion, familiar to every intelligent
traveller, in which the mind seems to swallow the sum
total of its impressions at a gulp. You take in the whole
place, whatever it be . . . .You feel England, you feel Italy,
and the sensation involves for the moment
a kind of thrill.

Henry James (1843-1916) American novelist

Know where you are if you later want to know
where you have been.

Caskie Stinnett (b. 1911) American writer,
***Grand and Private Pleasures,* 1977**

Look here
You've never seen this country
It's not the way you thought it was
Look again.

Al Purdy (b. 1918) Canadian poet

The difference between landscape and landscape
is small, but there is a great difference between
the beholders.

Ralph Waldo Emerson (1803-1882)
American essayist, poet, philosopher,
***Essays—Nature,* 1844**

Our journey was not dependent on the places we
found, but on how we chose to see them.

Christina Hardyment, English writer, *Heidi's Alp:*
***One Family's Search for Storybook Europe,* 1987**

80

Getting There

"How do you get to Neverland?" Wendy asked.
"Second star to the right, and straight on till morning."

**Sir James M. Barrie (1860–1937) British novelist,
dramatist, *Peter Pan,* 1904**

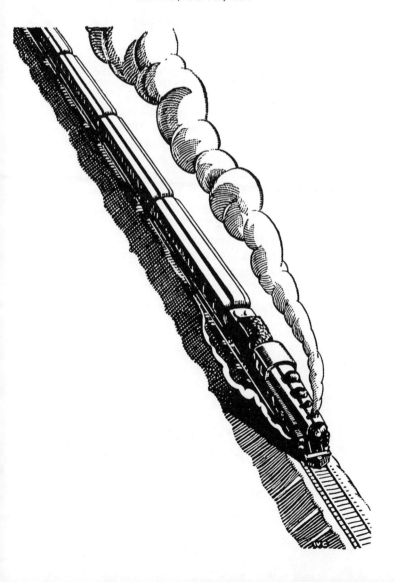

All travelling becomes dull in exact proportion
to its rapidity.

**John Ruskin (1819-1900) English critic, social
theorist, *Modern Painters***

Automobiles, planes, sometimes trains—In the modern
world they take us efficiently from here to there; they
also insulate us from the sounds, smells, and scenes of
everything in between.

**Shirley Deeter, American writer,
AdvenTOURing, 1991**

Going from point to point in other countries, one follows
a thin line of road, railway, or river, leaving wide tracts
unexplored on either side.

**Amelia Edwards (1831-1892) English journalist,
novelist, *A Thousand Miles Up the Nile*, 1877**

Mileage craziness is a serious condition that exists in
many forms. It can hit unsuspecting travelers while
driving cars, motorcycles, riding in planes, crossing the
country on bicycles or on foot. The symptoms may lead
to obsessively placing more importance on how many
miles are traveled than on the real reason for traveling.

Peter Jenkins (b. 1951) American writer, student

Whenever I travel I like to keep the seat next to me
empty. I found a great way to do it. When someone
walks down the aisle and says to you, "Is someone
sitting there?" just say, "no one—except the Lord."

Carol Leifer (20th c.) American writer

Roads

What is more beautiful than a road? It is the symbol and the image of an active, varied life.

George Sand (1804-1876) French novelist

You know more of a road by having traveled it than by all the conjectures and descriptions in the world.

William Hazlitt (1778-1830) English writer

I was going to stay on the three million miles of bent and narrow rural American two-lane, the roads to Podunk and Toonerville. Into the sticks, the boondocks, the burgs, backwaters, jerkwaters, the wide-spots-in-the-road, the don't-blink-or-you'll-miss-it towns. Into those places where you say, "My god! What if you lived here!" The Middle of Nowhere.

William Least Heat-Moon (b. 1939) American writer, *Blue Highways*, 1982

Road: a strip of ground over which one walks. A highway differs from a road not only because it is solely intended for vehicles, but also because it is merely a line that connects one point with another. A highway has no meaning in itself; its meaning derives entirely from the two points that it connects. A road is a tribute to space. Every stretch of road has meaning in itself and invites us to stop. A highway is the triumphant devaluation of space, which thanks to it has been reduced to a mere obstacle to human movement and a waste of time.

Milan Kundera (b. 1929) Czechoslovakian novelist, *Immortality*, 1990

Walking

. . . the swiftest traveller is he that goes afoot.

**Henry David Thoreau (1817-1862) American
poet, essayist, philosopher, *Walden*, 1854**

There is an expression—walking with beauty. And I
believe that this endless search for beauty in
surroundings, in people and one's personal life, is the
headstone of travel.

**Juliette de Bairacli Levy (b. 1937) British-born
wandering herbalist, writer, *Traveler's Joy*, 1979**

No one walks in Los Angeles—it's an old story, but I'll tell
it again—no one walks in Los Angeles!

**Spalding Gray (b. 1941) American monologuist,
writer, actor, *Monster in a Box*, 1991**

Restore human legs as a means of travel.
Pedestrians rely on food for fuel and need no special
parking facilities.

Lewis Mumford (b. 1895) American writer

It is good to collect things, but it is better to go on walks.

Anatole France (1844-1924) French novelist

Thus if one just keeps on walking,
everything will be all right.

**Sören Kierkegaard (1813-1855)
Danish philosopher**

. . . in Sherpa-country every track is marked with cairns
and prayer-flags, reminding you that Man's real home is
not a house, but the Road, and that life itself is a
journey to be walked on foot.

**Bruce Chatwin (1942-1989) British travel writer,
novelist, *What Am I Doing Here?*, 1989**

Elephants and Camels

He who mounts a wild elephant
goes where the wild elephant goes.

Randolph Bourne (1886–1918) American writer

A camel makes an elephant feel like a jet plane.

**Jacqueline Kennedy Onassis (b. 1929) American
former First Lady of The United Sates, editor**

Stagecoaches

There is a certain relief in change, even though it be
from bad to worse; as I have found in travelling in a
stage-coach, that it is often a comfort to shift one's
position and be bruised in a new place.

Washington Irving (1783–1859) American author

Rafts

We said there warn't no home like a raft, after all. Other
places do seem so cramped up and smothery, but a raft
don't. You feel mighty free and easy and comfortable
on a raft.

**Mark Twain (1835–1910) American author,
Adventures of Huckleberry Finn, 1884**

Ships and Sailing

My road leads me seaward to white dipping sails.

**John Masefield (1878-1967) British poet,
playwright, journalist**

Down at Ala Wai harbor it was all so different. I loved
the smell of rope and resin, even of diesel oil. I loved the
sound of water slapping hulls, the whip of halyards
against tall masts. These were the scents and sounds
of liberty and life.

**Robin Lee Graham (b. 1949) American sailor,
Dove, 1972**

The sight of a ship that was moving away like a
nocturnal traveller gave me the same impression that I
had had in the train of being set free from the
neccessity of sleep and from confinement in a bedroom.

**Marcel Proust (1871-1922) French novelist,
"Seascape, with Frieze of Girls,"
Remembrance of Things Past, 1936**

A solitary sail that rises
White in the blue mist on the foam—
What is it in far lands it prizes?
What does it leave behind at home?

**Mikhail Yurievich Lermontov (1814-1841)
Russian poet, "A Sail"**

The sea has never been friendly to man. At most it has
been the accomplice of human restlessness.

**Joseph Conrad (1857-1924) Polish-born British
novelist, *The Mirror of the Sea,* 1906**

*La mer promet monts et merveilles;
Fiez-vous-y, les vents el les voleurs viendront.*

The ocean promises mountains and marvels, but
beware! there are tempests and pirates as well.

**Jean de La Fontaine (1621-1695) French poet,
*Le Berger et la Mer***

GETTING THERE

I love to sail forbidden seas, and land
on barbarous coasts.

Herman Melville (1819-1891) American novelist,
***Moby Dick*, 1851**

. . . the sea was marvellously high, uneven, and crooked,
my appetite was slim, and for a time I postponed
cooking. (Confidentially, I was seasick!)

Captain Joshua Slocum (1844-1909) Nova Scotian
sailor, *Sailing Alone Around the World*, 1899

The only cure for seasickness is to sit on the shady side
of an old church in the country.

Anonymous

You never enjoy the world aright, till the sea itself
floweth in your veins, till you are clothed with the
heavens, and crowned with the stars . . .

Thomas Traherne (c. 1637-1674) English poet,
***Centuries of Meditations*, 1908**

He who rides the sea of the Nile
must have sails woven of patience. [Reis Shasli]

William Golding (1911-1993) English novelist,
***An Egyptian Journal*, 1985**

He was a seaman, but he was a wanderer, too, while
most seamen lead, if one may so express it, a sedentary
life. Their minds are of the stay-at-home order, and their
home is always with them–the ship; and so is their
country–the sea. One ship is very much like another,
and the sea is always the same. In the immutability of
their surroundings the foreign shores, the foreign faces,
the changing immensity of life, glide past, veiled not by
a sense of mystery but by a slightly disdainful
ignorance; for there is nothing mysterious to a seaman
unless it be the sea itself, which is the mistress of his
existence and as inscrutable as Destiny.

Joseph Conrad (1857-1924) Polish-born British
novelist, *Heart of Darkness*, 1910

FLINGING MONKEYS AT THE COCONUTS

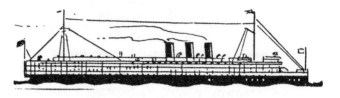

Give me this glorious ocean life, this salt-sea life, this briny, foamy life, when the sea neighs and snorts, and you breathe the very breath that the great whales respire! Let me roll around the globe, let me rock upon the sea; let me race and pant out my life, with an eternal breeze astern, and an endless sea before!

Herman Melville (1819-1891) American novelist,
Redburn

But O the ship, the immortal ship!
O ship aboard the ship!
Ship of the body, ship of the soul,
voyaging, voyaging, voyaging.

Walt Whitman (1819-1892) American poet,
Leaves of Grass

. . . the sea, once it casts its spell,
holds one in its net of wonder forever.

Jacques Yves Cousteau (b.1919) French author,
oceanographer, ***Life and Death in a Coral Sea,*** **1971**

A ship in the harbour is safe, but that is not
what ships are built for.

William Shedd (1820-1894) American professor
of English literature

I must go down to the seas again
To the lonely sea and the sky
And all I ask is a tall ship
And a star to steer her by.

John Masefield (1878-1967) British poet,
playwright, journalist, writer, "Sea Fever,"
Salt-Water Ballads, **1902**

One does not discover new lands without consenting to
lose sight of the shore for a very long time.

André Gide (1869-1951) French novelist, ***The***
Counterfeiters, **1926**

Trains

Never has man produced a more lonely sound than the whistle of a steam locomotive. It was a sad sound that seemed to say to each of us who heard it: 'Come with me and I'll show you America.'

**Hood River Blackie (b. 1926) American hobo,
"Home on the Rails,"** *Quest Magazine,*
Aug./Sept., 1978

My heart is warm with the friends I make,
And better friends I'll not be knowing;
Yet there isn't a train I wouldn't take,
No matter where it's going.

**Edna St. Vincent Millay (1892-1950) American
poet, "Travel,"** *Second April,* **1921**

Railway termini. They are our gates to the glorious and the unknown. Through them we pass out into adventure and sunshine, to them, alas! we return.

**E. M. Forster (1879-1970) English novelist,
Howards End, 1910**

It's still an emotional sort of place, an unforgettable crossroads for any traveler, where shoppers from suburbia mix with international businessmen, where kids with buckets and spades mingle with passengers for the Orient Express and where city gents carrying brollies step over more colorful travelers carrying guitars. Spend the morning here and you'll see every stereotype on earth.

**Mark Wallington, British writer, on London's
Victoria Station,** *In Britain,* **January 1984**

The only way to be sure of catching a train is to miss the one before it.

**G. K. Chesterton (1874-1936) English writer, qtd.
in P. Daninos,** *Vacances a Tous Prix,* **1958**

Just being in a train and rushing on to somewhere is extraordinarily nerve-soothing.

**Frank Tatchell (fl. 1920) English clergyman,
The Happy Traveller: A Book for Poor Men, 1923**

FLINGING MONKEYS AT THE COCONUTS

Herein, I think, is the chief attraction of railway travel.
The speed is so easy, and the train disturbs so little the
scenes through which it takes us, that our heart
becomes full of the placidity and stillness
of the country ...

**Robert Louis Stevenson (1850–1894) Scottish
novelist, poet, *Ordered South***

A third-class carriage is a community, while a first-class
carriage is a place of wild hermits.

**G. K. Chesterton (1874–1936) English novelist,
Heretics, 1905**

As you rock around helplessly at 4 a.m.,
you can't help marvelling at the infinite variety of
sounds a railway carriage can create—rattles, creaks,
thumps, squeals, grinds, jangles and pulses for which
there is no vocabulary.

**David Dale, Australian journalist, travel writer,
The Obsessive Traveller, 1991**

Anything is possible on a train: a great meal, a binge,
a visit from card players, an intrigue, a good night's
sleep, and strangers' monologues framed like Russian
short stories.

**Paul Theroux (b. 1941) American novelist, travel
writer, *The Great Railway Bazaar: By Train
through Asia,* 1975**

Going by railroad I do not consider as travelling at all; it
is merely being 'sent' to a place, and very little different
from becoming a parcel.

**John Ruskin (1819–1900) English critic, social
theorist, *Modern Painters***

It was a horrible train. But that was not a bad thing. It is
almost axiomatic that the worst trains take you through
magical places.

**Paul Theroux (b. 1941) American novelist, travel
writer, *Riding the Iron Rooster,* 1988**

Bicycles

The bicycle is the most civilised conveyance known to man. Other forms of transport grow daily more nightmarish. Only the bicycle remains pure in heart.

Iris Murdoch (b. 1919) Irish novelist

Bike riders are close to all of nature. They know what a mountain really is, or what a thirty-knot wind means, or how far fifty miles stretches out.

William Quinn, American cyclist, during 1979 solo bicycle trip across the United States at age sixty-two, qtd. in James C. Simmons,*The Big Book of Adventure Travel,* 1990

Bicycle touring is travel's live theater.

Tom Hale, founder of Backroads Bicycle Touring, qtd. in James C. Simmons, *The Big Book of Adventure Travel,* 1990

Motorcycles

You see things vacationing on a motorcycle in a way that is completely different from any other. In a car you're always in a compartment, and because you're used to it you don't realize that through that car window everything you see is just more TV. You're a passive observer and it is all moving by you boringly in a frame.

Robert M. Pirsig (b. 1928) American writer, *Zen and the Art of Motorcycle Maintenance,* 1974

Buses and Taxis

Sightseeing behind the tinted windows of a coach
severs man from nature.

Yi-Fu Tuan (b. 1930) Chinese geographer,
***Topophilia*, 1974**

It is such a bewildered, scared feeling to go
for the first time to a place and not know where to call
out to the driver to stop.

Katherine Butler Hathaway (1890–1942)
American author, *Journal and Letters of the Little
Locksmith*, 1943

The road to hell is thick with taxicabs.

Don Herold (1905–1960) American humorist

WE'RE OFF TO SEE
This Amazing America!"

Automobiles

Thanks to the Interstate Highway System,
it is now possible to travel from coast to coast
without seeing anything.

**Charles Kuralt (b. 1934) American journalist, T.V.
news correspondent, *On the Road,* 1985**

Tips on TRAVEL

... Americans drive across the country
as if someone's chasing them.

**Calvin Trillin (b. 1935) American author,
journalist, *Travels with Alice,* 1989**

To give you an idea how fast we traveled:
we left Spokane with two rabbits and when we got to
Topeka, we still had only two.

Bob Hope (b. 1903) American comedian

Always pee before a long car trip.

Martin Mull (b. 1943) American comedian

To look, really look out upon the world as it is framed
in the window of a moving vehicle
is to become a child again.

Anonymous

The car trip can draw the family together, as it was in
the days before television when parents and children
actually talked to each other.

Andrew H. Malcolm (b. 1943) American journalist

A love of crossing state lines. . . . We'd play license plate
games, and getting a Delaware in Oregon or a Nevada in
South Carolina or a Hawaii anywhere would spread a
happy mist of destiny over the rest of the day.

**Mark Winegardner (b. 1961) American writer,
Elvis Presley Boulevard, 1987**

MONTANA

Whither goest thou, America,
in thy shiny car in the night?

**Jack Kerouac (1922-1969) American poet,
novelist, _On the Road,_ 1957**

Are we there yet?

**Anonymous children, from post-World War II
nuclear family in car**

The more you ask how much longer it will take, the
longer the journey seems.

Maori proverb

Hitchhiking

Hitch-hiking is the art of wondering what will happen to
you between your starting point and your destination
and taking from everything that _does_ happen
everything that you can. . . . And unless you really have
to go somewhere, a destination is not all that
important. You can set out from London to go to Rome
and end up in Lisbon and what the hell?

Ken Welsh, _Hitch-hikers's Guide to Europe,_ 1971

The sweep of your skinny arm seems to last for
minutes. And even then you are passed by. But
no—brake lights!

**Tom Robbins (b. 1936) American writer, _Even
Cowgirls Get the Blues,_ 1976**

Hitchhiking, among its other virtues,
forces you to converse with people you'd otherwise
cross the street to avoid.

**Tony Horwitz (b. 1958) American journalist,
_One for the Road: Hitchhiking through the
Australian Outback,_ 1987**

Balloons

Balloonists have an unsurpassed view of the scenery,
but there is always the possibility that it may collide
with them.

**H. L. Mencken (1880-1956) American journalist,
The Bend in the Tube**

Airplanes

Whenever possible, avoid airlines which have
anyone's first name in their titles,
like Bob's International Airline or Air Fred.

**Miss Piggy, American Muppet, *Miss Piggy's
Guide to Life (As Told to Henry Beard)*, 1981**

Jet lag is for amateurs.

Dick Clark (b. 1929) host of *American Bandstand*

Never play peek-a-boo with a child on a long plane trip.
There's no end to the game. Finally I grabbed him by
the bib and said, "Look, it's always gonna be me!"

Rita Rudner (20th c.) American comediene

Though a plane is not the ideal place really to think, to
reassess or reevaluate things, it is a great place to have
the illusion of doing so, and often the illusion will suffice.

Shana Alexander (b. 1925) American journalist

It was the most wonderful flight of my life.
I reclined in the plane in a happy daze, occasionally
glancing out the window just to remind myself of the
distances we were traveling.

**Stuart Stevens, American political consultant,
journalist, *Night Train to Turkistan*, 1988**

In seconds, the voice of the pilot, in the cowboy drawl
that even French pilots seem to employ, came on to say
something about turbulence, downdraft, and calm. We
sat back in our seats, strapped ourselves more closely
in, our blood humming, relishing the relief of still being
alive, still suspended, droning through the night. Now it
was as if our attention to flying was needed in order to
hold the airplane up . . .

**Diane Johnson (b. 1934) American novelist,
essayist, *Natural Opium*, 1992**

... we ride out to big airports and climb onto big planes
that are as amiably de-cultured as Muzak, as white
sound. The jumbo jet is the airborne equivalent of the
interstate highway—fast and convenient, but a sort of
whispering vacuum. . . . What happens to travel when it
consists of getting onto a big plane and eating a tray
dinner and having a drink and watching a movie? And
then getting off the plane at an airport much like the
one we left and riding to a big hotel and finding a room
where the toilet seat wears a preposterous paper sash
FOR YOUR SANITARY PROTECTION?

**Lance Morrow (b. 1939) American writer, "Is the
Going Still Good?,"** *Time,* **May 31, 1982**

Airline travel is hours of boredom interrupted by
moments of stark terror.

Al Boliska

... you define a good flight by negatives: you didn't get
highjacked, you didn't crash, you didn't throw up, you
weren't late, you weren't nauseated by the food.
So you are grateful.

**Paul Theroux (b. 1941) American novelist, travel
writer,** *The Old Patagonian Express,* **1979**

The wonders of air travel:
Breakfast in Paris
Lunch in New York
Dinner in San Francisco
Luggage in Rio

Fred Runyon

... air travel shrink-wraps the world leaving it small,
odourless, tidy and usually out of sight.

Michael Palin, British actor, comedian, writer,
Around the World in 80 Days, **1989**

Space Travel

. . . To explore strange new worlds
To seek out new civilisations,
To boldly go where no man has gone before . . .

James T. Kirk, captain of the Starship *Enterprise*

Treading the soil of the moon, palpitating its pebbles,
tasting the panic and splendour of the event, feeling in
the pit of one's stomach the separation from
terra–these form the most romantic sensations an
explorer has ever known.

**Vladimir Nabokov (1899-1977) Russian-born
American novelist, poet, in *The New York Times*,
July 21, 1969**

Time Travel

I am afraid I cannot convey the peculiar sensations of
time travelling. They were excessively unpleasant. There
is a feeling exactly like that one has upon a
switchback–of a helpless headlong motion! I felt the
same horrible anticipation, too, of an imminent smash.

**H. G. Wells (1866-1946) English author,
The Time Machine, 1895**

97

Nature

At the gates of the forest, the surprised man of the
world is forced to leave his city estimates
of great and small, wise and foolish. The knapsack of
custom falls off his back.

**Ralph Waldo Emerson (1803-1882) American
essayist, poet, philosopher, *Essays, Second
Series: Nature*, 1844**

FLINGING MONKEYS AT THE COCONUTS

The greatest practice for a traveler
is to meditate on nature.

Yogi Bhajan

Only by going alone in silence, without baggage, can
one truly get into the heart of the wilderness. All other
travel is mere dust and hotels and baggage and chatter.

**John Muir (1838-1914) Scottish-born American
naturalist, *The Life and Letters of John Muir,* 1924**

The skies and land are so enormous, the detail so
precise and exquisite, that wherever you are you are
isolated in a glowing world between the macro and the
micro, where everything is sidewise under, and over
you, and the clocks stopped long ago.

**Ansel Adams (1902-1984)
American photographer**

Mountains

The man who bivouacs becomes one with the
mountain. On his bed of stone, leaning against the great
wall, facing empty space which has become his friend,
he watches the sun fade over the horizon on his left,
while on his right the sky spreads its mantle of stars.

**Gaston Rébuffat (1921-1985) French
mountain-climbing guide, photographer,
Between Heaven and Earth, 1965**

On top we hugged each other with supreme joy. The air
was absolutely still and we stripped off jackets and
gloves. Glaciers and peaks extended out from us in all
directions, and for a few minutes we felt as if we were
in the center of the universe, perched on a cloud. We
might have rolled in the snow and burst out laughing
with complete emotional release, were it not for the
prospect of the descent, always in our minds.

**Galen Rowell (b.1940) American photographer,
mountain climber, essayist, *High and Wild,* 1983**

. . . it is not necessary to embrace the hills in order to
achieve happiness. It is true that full knowledge and
intimate contact is required if we are to receive in heart
and soul and mind all that they have to offer, but the
eager pilgrim will find contentment and an uplifting of
spirit even in the distant presence of the mountains.

**Sir Douglas Busk (b. 1906) English climber,
The Delectable Mountains, 1946**

But then, as one of my Japanese friends was fond of
saying, Fuji is only a 'seeing' mountain; it was never
meant to be climbed. The Japanese, however, have a
saying that there are two kinds of fool: those who have
never climbed Mount Fuji, and those who have climbed
it more than once.

**John Morris (1895-1980) English broadcaster,
Traveler from Tokyo, 1943**

. . . going to the mountains is going home.

**John Muir (1838-1914) Scottish-born American
conservationist, "Summering in the Sierra,"** *San
Francisco Daily Evening Bulletin,* **August 24, 1876**

My heart's in the Highlands wherever I go.

Robert Burns (1759-1796) Scottish poet

There are many ways to enjoy mountains: some
engage their passion by cutting steps into impossible
ice walls, others entrust their lives to one fragile piton in
a rocky crevice, and still others, I among them, prefer to
simply roam the high country.

George Schaller, American naturalist,
***The Stones of Silence,* 1979**

My father considered a walk among the mountains
as the equivalent of churchgoing.

Aldous Huxley (1894-1963) British novelist

Streams and Rivers

Les rivières sont des chemins qui marchent.
Rivers are moving roads.

Blaise Pascal (1623–1662) French philosopher,
Pensées, Adversaria

Only the river is free, always changing
but always the same . . .

Raymond Sokolov (b. 1941) American writer,
***Native Intelligence*, 1975**

Most streams appear to travel through a country with
thoughts and plans for something beyond. But those of
Florida are at home, do not appear to be traveling at all,
and seem to know nothing of the sea.

**John Muir (1838–1914) Scottish-born American
naturalist, *A Thousand-Mile Walk to the Gulf*, 1916**

Viam qui nescit, qua deveniat ad mare,
Eum oportet amnen quaerere comitem sibi.

If you don't know the way to the sea,
take a river as your travelling companion.

Poenulus

103

Islands and Beaches

Along the shore my hand is on its pulse,
And I converse with many a shipwrecked crew.

**Henry David Thoreau (1817–1862) American
poet, essayist, philosopher, "My Life Is Like a
Stroll upon the Beach," 1849**

The first experience can never be repeated. The first
love, the first sun-rise, the first South Sea Island, are
memories apart, and touched a virginity of sense.

**Robert Louis Stevenson (1850–1894) Scottish
novelist poet, *In the South Seas*, 1889**

Long lines of patient yearning palms keep faithful
rendezvous with faithless lover-winds beside the sea.

**Don Blanding (1894–1957) American poet,
Vagabond House, 1928**

As one who sits ashore and longs perchance
To visit dolphin-coral in deep seas.

**John Keats (1795–1821) British romantic poet,
"To Homer," 1818**

Of Paradise can I not speak properly,
for I have not been there.

**John Mandevile (c. 1322–c. 1372) British author,
The Book of John Manndevile, c. 1360**

The longing for paradise is paradise itself.

**Kahlil Gibran (1883–1931) Lebanese mystic poet,
novelist, *Spiritual Sayings*, 1963**

Deserts

The desert is an ocean upon which we can walk,
it is the image of immensity.

**Napoleon Bonaparte (1769–1821) French
emperor, *Political Aphorisms, Moral and
Philosophical Thoughts of the Emperor Napoleon*,
Cte. Ate. G. De Liancourt, ed.**

I was crossing the desert. Smooth. Wind rippling at the
window. There was no road, only alkaline plain. There
was no reason for me to be steering; I let go of the
wheel. There was no reason to sit where I was; I moved
to the opposite seat. I stared at the empty driver's seat.

**Barry Lopez (b. 1945) American naturalist writer,
Desert Notes, 1976**

White sheets of mirage, like a shallow lake country far
away, melt in the horizon, run into each other,
recede as we approach.

**Freya Stark (b. 1893) French-born English travel
writer, photographer, *Baghdad Sketches,* 1929**

He will carry, however faint, the imprint of the desert,
the brand which marks the nomad; and he will have
within him the yearning to return, weak or insistent
according to his nature. For this cruel land can cast a
spell which no temperate clime can match.

**Wilfred Thesiger (b. 1910) Ethiopian-born English
explorer, photographer, *Arabian Sands,* 1959**

Not to have known either the mountain or the desert is not to have known one's self. Not to have known oneself is to have known no one.

**Joseph Wood Krutch (1893-1970)
American essayist**

Was that what travel meant? An exploration of the deserts of memory, rather than those around me?

**Claude Lévi-Strauss (b. 1908) French
anthropologist,** *Tristes Tropiques,* **1955**

Once I asked a Papago youngster what the desert smelled like to him. He answered with little hesitation:

"The desert smells like rain."

Gary Paul Nabhan, *The Desert Smells Like Rain,* **1982**

There is something infectious about the magic of the Southwest. Some are immune to it, but there are others who have no resistance to the subtle lures and who must spend the rest of their lives dreaming of the incredible sweep of the desert, of great golden mesas with purple shadows, and tremendous stars appearing at dusk from a turquoise sky. Once infected, there is nothing one can do but strive to return again and again.

**H. M. Wormington (b. 1914) American
archaeologist,** *Prehistoric Indians of the
Southwest,* **1959**

Climate and Weather

The traveller must be born again on the road, and earn
a passport from the elements.

**Henry David Thoreau (1817-1862) American
poet, essayist, philosopher**

Climate is what you expect. Weather is what you get.

Anonymous

People get a bad impression of it [the English climate]
by continually trying to treat it as if it was a bank clerk,
who ought to be on time on Tuesday next, instead of
philosophically seeing it as a painter, who may do
anything so long as you don't try to predict what.

**Katherine Whitehorn (b. 1926) British journalist,
The Observer, August 7, 1966**

Part of travel is about memories, but the more
important part may be about forgetting. Some things,
because they are so wonderful, are too painful to
remember. The best example, I think, is the weather
in Los Angeles.

**Richard Reeves (b. 1936) American journalist,
Travel & Leisure, October 1991**

. . . When I heard the storm I made haste to join it;
for in storms nature has always something
extra fine to show us.

**John Muir (1838-1914) Scottish-born American
naturalist, wilderness conservationist, "An
Adventure with a Dog and a Glacier," _Century
Magazine_, September 1897, _Stickeen_, 1909**

As a nomad you are in closer tune with the
environment: up to watch the sunrise and every dinner
wrapped in a sunset. Each full moon is something to
celebrate. Each day is an odyssey in adventure and
every night is a challenge to find another more
intriguing campsite.

**Stephen Lee Arrington, American surfer, "Jail
Bars and Gypsy Lifestyles," _Surfer Magazine_,
May 1984**

FLINGING MONKEYS AT THE COCONUTS

The weather is grey and stormy and dark.
Where am I going?

**Isabelle Eberhardt (1877-1932) Swiss traveler,
on departure form Geneva, July 14, 1900,
*The Passionate Nomad***

San Diego

Sun

Red sky in morning, sailors take warning
Red sky at night, sailors delight

Maritime saying

The Sun himself cannot forget
His fellow traveller.

**Anonymous English, on Sir Francis Drake, *Wit's
Recreations,* 1640, Epigrams, No. 146**

It was hot now: the kind of heat you can hear.

**Jeremy Harding, English writer, in the Western
Sahara, "Polisario," *Granta* 26, Spring 1989**

Shipwrecked, the sun sinks down
harbours of a sky, unloads its liquid cargo
of marigolds.

**Dannie Abse (b. 1923) British poet, novelist,
playwright, physician, "Epihalamion,"
Walking Under Water, 1952**

I was a vagabond; sunset and moon
Found me a place in their hearts.

**Lawrence Durrell (1912-1990) Indian-born
British novelist poet, "Happy Vagabond," 1930**

Night, Stars and Moon

I know nothing, nothing in the world, equal to the
wonder of nightfall in the air.

**Antoine De Saint-Exupéry (1900-1944) French
author, aviator, *Wind, Sand, and Stars*, 1939**

The night is dark, and I am far from home.

**John Henry Newman (1801-1890) English poet,
novelist, clergyman, *Lead, Kindly Light*, 1833**

'Is there anybody there?' said the traveller,
Knocking on the moonlit door.

**Walter de la Mare (1873, 1956) English romantic
poet, novelist, anthologist, *The Listeners*, 1912**

A star shall be our pilot
Across the sea of light,
And some enchanted island
Shall be our port at night.

Edith M. Thomas (1854-1925) American poet

It is the stars not known to science that I would know,
the stars which the lonely traveler knows.

**Henry David Thoreau (1817-1862) American
poet, essayist, philosopher**

The Moon, that traveller's friend, a companion to the
solitary man, like the blazing hearth of Northern
climates, rose behind the filmy tree-tops and made us
hail the gentle light.

**Sir Richard Francis Burton (1821-1890) English explorer,
Explorations of the Highlands of the Brazil, 1869**

The moon was a ghostly galleon
tossed upon cloudy seas,
The road was a ribbon of moonlight
over the purple moor . . .

**Alfred Noyes (1880-1958) British poet,
"The Highwayman," *Forty Singing Seamen and
Other Poems*, 1907**

O' white moon, you are lonely
It is the same with me,
But we have the world to roam over,
Only the lonely are free.

**Sara Teasdale (1884–1933) American poet,
"Morning Song," 1907**

We had become, with the approach of night, once
more aware of loneliness and time
those two companions without whom no journey can
yield us anything.

**Lawrence Durrell (1912–1990) Indian-born
British novelist, poet, *Bitter Lemons,* 1957**

Chicago

Wind and Clouds

*Nullius addictus iurare in verba magistri,
Quo me cumque rapit tempestas, deferor hospes.*

Not bound to swear allegiance to any master,
wherever the wind
takes me I travel as a visitor.

Horace (65 –8 B.C.) Roman poet, satirist, *Epistles*

Winds are advertisements of all they touch . . . telling
their wanderings even by their scents alone.

**John Muir (1838–1914) Scottish-born American
naturalist, "A Wind Storm in the Forests of the
Yuba," *Scribner's Monthly,* November 1879**

The moon is a great gold coin tossed
to those ragged vagabonds, the clouds.

**Don Blanding (1897–1957) American poet,
Vagabond House, 1928**

Rain and Snow

I'm leaving because the weather is too good.
I hate London when it's not raining.

Groucho Marx (1895-1977) American comedian,
British News Summaries, June 28, 1954

A rainy day is the perfect time for a walk in the woods.

Rachel Carson (1907-1964) American marine
biologist, author *The Sense of Wonder*, 1956

A cold coming we had of it,
Just the worst time of the year
For a journey, and such a long journey:
The ways deep and the weather sharp,
The very dead of winter.

T. S. Eliot (1888-1965) American-born English
poet, "Journey of the Magi," *Ariel Poems*, 1927

By the time I crossed the frontier from Mongolia into
Irkutsk the temperature was so low you would have
required to get down on your hands and knees to see it.

James Cameron (1911-1985) British journalist,
***Points of Departure*, 1967**

"Cleveland," a friend wrote to her in the midst of a blizzard, "is a place I have visited only in jokes."

Tony Horwitz (b. 1958) American journalist,
One for the Road: Hitchhiking through the
Australian Outback, **1987**

Wonderful to go out on a frozen road. . . . Wonderful the bluish, cold air, and things standing up in cold distance. . . . I am so glad, on this lonely naked road, I don't know what to do with myself.

D. H. Lawrence (1885–1930) English novelist,
Sea and Sardinia, **1921**

A traveller, by the faithful hound,
Half-buried in the snow was found.

Henry Wadsworth Longfellow (1807–1882)
American poet, *Excelsior*

Travelling is a cold business.

Anton Chekhov (1860–1904) Russian dramatist,
in Siberia, May 14, 1890, *The Selected Letters of*
Anton Chekhov, **1955**

Adventure and Adversity

As much trouble as I've had on this little journey, I'm
sure one day I'm going to look back and laugh.

**Steve Martin (b. 1945) American comedian,
actor,** *Planes, Trains and Automobiles,* **1987**

There is nothing like a comfortable adventure
to put people in a good humor . . .

Peter Mayle, English writer, *Toujours Provence*, 1991

Adventure is my only reason for living.

**Alexandra David-Neel (1868-1969) French
journalist, explorer**

When you're safe at home you wish you were having
an adventure; when you're having an adventure you
wish you were safe at home.

**Thornton Wilder (1897-1975)
American novelist, playwright**

At stressful moments in travel, I try to console myself
with worse moments elsewhere.

**Martha Gellhorn (b. 1908) American novelist, short-story
writer, "White into Black," *Granta* 10, 1984**

Travel is a foretaste of hell.

Turkestan proverb

Adversity is the first path to truth.

**Lord Byron (1788-1824) British romantic poet,
Don Juan, 1819-24**

We must travel in the direction of our fear.

**John Berryman (1914-1972) American poet,
"A Point of Age," *Poems*, 1942**

I haven't yet learned to be careful in travel.

**Martha Gellhorn (b. 1908) American novelist, short-story
writer, "White into Black," *Granta* 10, 1984**

WASHINGTON

But travel is work. Etymologically a traveler is one who suffers travail, a word deriving in its turn from Latin tripalium, a torture instrument consisting of three stakes designed to rack the body.

Paul Fussell (b. 1924) American professor of English literature, *Abroad*, 1980

Travel is glamorous only in retrospect.

Paul Theroux (b. 1941) American novelist, travel writer, qtd. in *The Observer*, October 7, 1979

All at once the Land Rover came to a halt with a clank. . . . One of the laws of travel is that there must always be a breakdown there is even something reassuring about it, some assertion of natural law reminding that the world is in order.

Diane Johnson (b. 1934) American novelist, essayist, *Natural Opium*, 1992

To lose a passport was the least of one's worries: to lose a notebook was a catastrophe.

Bruce Chatwin (1942-1989) British travel writer, novelist, *The Songlines*, 1987

Real travel in itself is often a matter of life and death—or at least I've thought so. One makes instant alliances on the spot to stave the latter off. I generally arrive by air, in the modern manner, but without plans or reservations and usually after dark in a city like Dar es Salaam or Cairo or Khartoum, to see what happens and lend my first impressions an old-fashioned immediacy. Then I go by bus or truck or train. In Eskimo villages at 40-below I have simply put myself at the mercy of the residents: help me or I'll die. A selfish but effective method of learning how they live.

Edward Hoagland (b. 1932) American novelist, travel writer, essayist, *Letter on Travel*

Part of the urge to explore is a desire to become lost.

Tracy Johnston, American writer, *Shooting the Boh*, 1992

NEW ZEALAND

FLINGING MONKEYS AT THE COCONUTS

I wasn't lost, I just didn't know where I was
for a few weeks.

Jim Bridger, 19th-c American frontiersman

There are three wants which can never be satisfied:
that of the rich, who wants something more; that of the
sick, who wants something different, and that of the
traveller, who says "Anywhere but here."

**Ralph Waldo Emerson (1803–1882) American
poet, philosopher, essayist, "Considerations by
the Way," *The Conduct of Life,* 1860**

There is a special ambivalence to journeys in which
one's own discomfort seems mitigated by an
awareness of the much greater misery of the people
around one—though that mitigation adds another
dimension of discomfort, the mental spasm of guilt.

**George Woodcock (b. 1912) Canadian poet,
"My Worst Journeys," *Bad Trips,* 1991,
Keath Fraser, ed.**

What am I doing here?

**Arthur Rimbaud (1854–1891) French poet,
writing home from Ethiopia**

Where the heck am I, anyway? . . . Well, wherever it is, I
don't like it and I'm gettin' outta here.

**Bugs Bunny (20th c.) American rabbit,
*The Bugs Bunny Show***

Should we have stayed at home and thought of here?

**Elizabeth Bishop (1911–1979) American-born
Brazilian poet, "Questions of Travel," 1965**

En largo camino paja pesa.

On a long journey even a straw weighs heavy.

Spanish proverb

It is not the path which is the difficulty; rather, it is the
difficulty which is the path.

**Sören Kierkegaard (1813–1855)
Danish philosopher**

ADVENTURE AND ADVERSITY

The road uphill
and the road downhill
are one and the same.

Heraclitus (c. 540-480 B.C.) Greek philosopher

An irksome drudgery seems it to plod on,
Through hot and dusty ways, or pelting storm,
A vagrant merchant under a heavy load
Bent as he moves, and needing frequent rest;
Yet do such travellers find their own delight . . .

**William Wordsworth (1770-1850) English
romantic poet, "The Excursion"**

When you have gone so far that you can't manage
one more step, then you've gone just half the distance
that you're capable of.

Greenland proverb

. . . you must go on, I can't go on, I'll go on.

**Samuel Beckett (b. 1906) Irish novelist, poet,
playwright, *The Unnamable*, 1959**

. . . For afterwards a man finds pleasure in his pains,
when he has suffered long and wandered long.

Homer (c. 700 B.C.) Greek poet

*Centum solatia curae Et rus,
et comites, et via longa dabit.*

The country, your companions, and the length
of your journey will afford a hundred
compensations for your toil.

**Ovid (43 B.C.-A.D.) Roman poet,
*Remediorum Amoris***

One always begins to forgive a place
as soon as it's left behind.

Charles Dickens (1812-1870) English novelist

One does not love a place the less for having suffered in
it unless it has all been suffering, nothing but suffering.

**Jane Austen (1775-1817) English novelist,
Persuasion, 1818**

FLINGING MONKEYS AT THE COCONUTS

Visits always give pleasure
if not the arrival, the departure.

Portuguese proverb

No matter what happens, travel gives you a story to tell.

Jewish proverb

The only aspect of our travels that is guaranteed
to hold an audience is disaster.

**Martha Gellhorn (b. 1908) American novelist,
short-story writer, *Travels with Myself and
Another,* 1978**

Let the tourist be cushioned against misadventure; but
your true traveller will not feel that he has had his
money's worth unless he brings back a few scars . . .

**Lawrence Durrell (1912–1990) Indian-born
British novelist, "Reflections on Travel," *Sunday
Times* (London) December 27, 1959**

Travelling may be one of two things
an experience we shall always remember, or an
experience which, alas, we shall never forget.

**J. Gordon (1896–1952) English writer,
Your Sense of Humor, 1930**

Toto, I've a feeling we're not in Kansas anymore.

**Judy Garland (1922–1969) American actress, as
Dorothy in *The Wizard of Oz,* 1939**

Adventure is not in the guidebook
and Beauty is not on the map.

**Terry and Renny Russell, American authors,
On the Loose, 1967**

Travel stripped of adventure is almost inevitably
an exercise imbedded in monotony;
without it the traveler moves through strange lands
untouched and touching nothing.

**Caskie Stinnett (b. 1911) American writer, *Grand
and Private Pleasures,* 1977**

Return and Reentry

Sailing round the world
in a dirty gondola
Oh to be back in the land
of Coca-Cola!

Bob Dylan (b.1941) American singer, composer

Leaving a Place

I have before seen other countries, in the same manner,
give themselves to you when you are
about to leave them.

**Isak Dinesen (1885–1962) Danish author,
Out of Africa, 1937**

GREECE

I think wherever you go becomes
a part of you somehow.

**Anita Desai (b. 1937) Indian novelist, "Frozen in
Frøya," *Bad Trips*, 1991, Keath Fraser, ed.**

You see, I hadn't had a Perfect Moment yet, and I always
like to have one before I leave an exotic place. They're a
good way of bringing things to an end. But you can
never plan for one. You never know when they're
coming. It's sort of like falling in love . . . with yourself.

**Spalding Gray (b. 1941) American monologuist, writer,
actor, in Thailand, *Swimming to Cambodia*, 1985**

. . . time manages the most painful partings for us. One
has only to set the date, buy the ticket, and let the
earth, sun, and moon make their passages through the
sky, until inexorable time carries us with it to the
moment of parting.

**Jill Ker Conway (b. 1933) Australian scholar,
The Road from Coorain, 1989**

Oregon

In a few weeks I will get on to an aeroplane and fly, like
a bird, like a god, across continents and oceans, across
summer and winter, across night and day, across the
world so that I can see his face again.

**Susan Pointon, Australian writer, "Framed,"
Home and Away, 1987, Rosemary Creswell, ed.**

120

One of the difficulties of my trip was this continual saying goodby to friends. I was never in one place long enough to enjoy a sustained friendship, and I found that frustrating. I would meet someone I liked, and within a day we could be great friends. The next day I might be gone. The knowledge that I would soon be leaving intensified the quality of the relationships. I wouldn't waste my time with people who didn't interest me or who were a drain on my energy. It was a valuable lesson. How quickly I fell back into bad habits when the trip was over.

Eric Hansen (b. 1948) American travel writer,
Stranger in the Forest, **1988**

I was sorry to leave; I had grown to like these people. Parting is sweet sorrow.

P. K. Page (b. 1916) English-born Canadian poet,
"On the Road Again: The Australian Outback,
June 1956,", *Bad Trips,* **1991, Keath Fraser, ed.**

Our battered suitcases were piled on the sidewalk again; we had longer ways to go. But no matter, the road is life.

Jack Kerouac (1922-1969) American
poet,novelist, *On the Road,* **1957**

A boat was leaving in about ten days and the knowledge that I would take that boat had already brought the journey to an end.

Henry Miller (1891-1980) American author,
The Colossus of Maroussi, **1941**

. . . I was also beginning to feel strangely let down. The trip was almost over, and all that was left was a predictable tapering away of the experience . . .

Tracy Johnston, American writer,
Shooting the Boh, **1992**

I love this place. When I am here, I think I would be happy never to leave it. Every trip has to end.

Charles Kuralt (b. 1934) American journalist,
A Life on the Road, **1990**

FLINGING MONKEYS AT THE COCONUTS

A true journey, no matter how long the travel takes,
has no end.

**William Least Heat-Moon (b. 1939) American
writer, *Blue Highways*, 1982**

Push not off from that isle; thou canst never return.

Herman Melville (1819-1891) American novelist

"I shall never see this again"
bobbed up and down inside of me.

**Jamaica Kincaid (b. 1949) Antiguan writer, on
leaving Antigua, *Annie John*, 1983**

Traveling is not just seeing the new; it is also leaving
behind. Not just opening doors; also closing them
behind you, never to return. But the place you have left
forever is always there for you to see whenever you
shut your eyes. And the cities you see most clearly at
night are the cities you have left and
will never see again.

**Jan Myrdal (b. 1927) Swedish essayist, novelist,
playwright, *The Silk Road*, 1979**

Goodbye and fare you well, for I am homeward bound.

**Mary Kingsley (1862-1900) English naturalist,
speaking to a London audience shortly before
her final African journey**

There's no place like home. . . .
There's no place like home. . . .

**Judy Garland (1922-1969) American actress, as
Dorothy in *The Wizard of Oz*, 1939**

How hard it is to escape from places!
However carefully one goes, they hold you
—you leave little bits of yourself fluttering on the fences,
little rags and shreds of your very life.

**Katherine Mansfield (1888-1923) New
Zealand-born British writer**

Homeward Bound

What a long strange trip it's been.

Grateful Dead, American band, "Truckin"

Besides the pleasures of revisiting, an important aspect of traveling is, to me at least, the journey back. Here, the time element does not much matter. A journey may last three days, three months, or one year, yet a traveler always becomes excited when his train or ship approaches his home destination.

Kin-ichi Ishikawa (1895-1959) Japanese journalist, "About Traveling," *A Book of Thoughts,* **1958**

Oh ! dream of joy ! is this indeed
The light-house top I see ?
Is this the hill ? is this the kirk ?
Is this mine own countree ?

Samuel Taylor Coleridge (1772-1834) English poet, "Rime of the Ancient Mariner," 1834

Like kites we have sailed on the wind
through many days and soon someone may tug us
and begin to wind us in, flicking a wrist back and forth
until we are home again.

Ann Woodin, American writer, *In the Circle of the Sun,* **1971**

FLINGING MONKEYS AT THE COCONUTS

Sometimes I saw what men
have only dreamed of seeing.

Arthur Rimbaud (1854–1891) French poet

Like all great travellers, I have seen more than I
remember, and remember more than I have seen.

Benjamin Disraeli (1804–1881) British statesman

It is a strange thing to come home. While yet on the
journey, you cannot all realize how strange it will be.

Selma Lagerlöf (1858–1940) Swedish writer

Here I am, safely returned over those peaks from a
journey far more beautiful and strange than anything I
had hoped for or imagined—how is it that this safe
return brings such regret?

**Peter Matthiessen (b. 1927) American naturalist,
novelist, *The Snow Leopard*, 1978**

Heureux qui, comme Ulysse, a fait un beau voyage
Happy he who like Ulysses has made a glorious voyage.

**Joachim du Bellay (1522–1560) French poet,
Les Regrets, 1559**

I traveled among unknown men,
In lands beyond the sea;
Nor, England! did I know till then
What love I bore to thee.

**William Wordsworth (1770–1850) English poet,
I Traveled Among Unknown Men, 1807**

Much have I travell'd in the realms of gold . . .

**John Keats (1795–1821) British romantic poet,
"On First Looking into Chapman's Homer," 1816**

Reflections at Home

The whole object of travel is not to set foot
on foreign land; it is at last to set foot on one's own
country as foreign land.

G. K. Chesterton (1874-1936) English novelist

This is one of the lessons of travel–that some of the
strangest races dwell next door to you at home.

**Robert Louis Stevenson (1850-1894) Scottish
novelist, poet, *Across the Plains***

You can also suffer from reverse culture shock when
you get home after a long trip!

David Else, British author, *Backpacker's Africa,* 1988

We have had an unspeakably delightful journey,
one of those journeys which seem to divide
one's life in two, by the new ideas they suggest
and the new views of interest they open.

George Eliot (1819-1880) British novelist

Travel has been my comrade, Adventure my inspiration,
Accomplishment my recompense.

**Charlotte Cameron (d. 1946)
English globetrotteress**

What had the voyage achieved besides making dreams
a reality? I probably think the most important thing it
had done for me was to enable me to stand back,
away from human society, and look ashore, and look at
life for a little while from a new perspective.

**Robert Manry (b. 1918) Indian-born American
sailor, *Tinkerbelle,* 1966**

FLINGING MONKEYS AT THE COCONUTS

. . . my journey around the world gave me a sense
of global scale, of the size and variety of this
extraordinary planet, of the relation of one country
and one culture to another which few people
experience and many ought to.

Michael Palin, British actor, comedian, writer,
***Around the World in 80 Days,* 1989**

Well, I learned a lot. You'd be surprised.
They're all individual countries.

**Ronald Reagan (b. 1911) American President
(1981-1989) actor, following his 1982 trip to
South America**

If an ass goes traveling he will not come home a horse.

**Thomas Fuller (1654-1734) English physician,
Gnomologia, 1732**

Travel is the most private of pleasures. There is no
greater bore than the travel bore. We do not in the least
want to hear what he has seen in Hong-Kong.

**Vita Sackville-West (1892-1962) English writer,
poet, *Passenger to Teheran,* 1926**

. . . slide projectors clicking in the dark to punctuate a
drone of travelogue. The oppressed audience writhes
and dozes and works its eyes open and shut like
jalousies. Etna will be seen in a bleeding, theatrical
sunset. . . . In some former slave-driving colony of the
Caribbean, Dwayne will lounge by the pool wearing
his Club Med drinking beads and a sun-dazed,
dreamy smile.

**Lance Morrow (b. 1939) American essayist, "Is
the Going Still Good?," *Time,* May 31, 1982**

The traveller who has gone to Italy to study the tactile
values of Giotto, or the corruption of the Papacy, may
return remembering nothing but the blue sky and the
men and women who live under it.

**E. M. Forster (1879-1970) English novelist, *A
Room with a View,* 1908**

Tips on TRAVEL

126

RETURN AND REENTRY

The things I remember most, for travel is all vanished remembered stories, story bits, are about food, sex, music, and houses. These things in combination are especially good.

Michelle Dominique Leigh (b. 1954) American writer, "The Blue-Green Seas of Forever," *The House on Via Gombito*, 1991, Madelon Sprengnether & C. W. Truesdale, eds.

But there is one priceless thing that I brought back from my trip around the world, one that cost no money and on which I paid no customs duty: humility, a humility born from watching other peoples, other races, struggling bravely and hoping humbly for the simplest things in life.

Félix Martí-Ibáñez (d.1972) Spanish-born American psychiatrist, *Journey Around Myself*, 1966

I met a lot of people in Europe.
I even encountered myself.

James Baldwin (1924-1987) American novelist

When a traveller returneth home, let him not leave the countries where he hath travelled altogether behind him, but maintain a correspondence by letters with those of his acquaintance which are of most worth.

Francis Bacon (1561–1626) English philosopher, *Essays*, 1597-1625

A man travels the world over in search of what he needs and returns home to find it.

George Moore (1852-1933) Irish writer, art critic, *The Brook Kerith*, 1916

'Mid pleasures and palaces
though we may roam,
Be it ever so humble,
there's no place like home.

John Howard Payne (1791-1852) American actor, dramatist, from the opera *Clari, the Maid of Milan*, 1823

Travelers are fantasists, conjurers—seers, and what
they finally discover is that every round object
everywhere is a crystal ball: stone, teapot, the
marvelous globe of the human eye.

**Cynthia Ozick (b. 1928) American novelist,
essayist, "Enchanters at First Encounter," *The
New York Times*, March 17, 1985**

We shall not cease from exploration
And the end of all our exploring
Will be to arrive where we started
And know the place for the first time.

**T. S. Eliot (1888–1965) American-born English
poet, "Little Gidding," *Four Quartets*, 1943**

Our journeying is a great-circle sailing.

**Henry David Thoreau (1817–1862) American
poet, essayist, philosopher**

Ah, what is more blessed than to put care aside,
when the mind lays down its burden, and spent with
distant travel, we come home again and rest on the
couch we longed for?

Catullus (c.87–54 B.C.) Roman poet, *Carmina*

He travelled in order to come home.

**William Trevor (b. 1928) Irish dramatist,
*Matilda's England***

Trips start when the last familiar face recedes from view,
and end the instant one reappears.

Lance Free, *The Art of Tripping*

Further Travels

I cannot rest from travel: I will drink
Life to the lees: all times I have enjoyed
Greatly, have suffered greatly, both with those
That loved me, and alone;
I am become a name;
For always roaming with a hungry heart
Much have I seen and known. . .

**Alfred Lord Tennyson (1809–1892) British poet,
Ulysses, 1842**

Home was to be a schooner in the South Seas, a raft in
Borneo, a tent on safari, a hut in the Congo, sometimes
a dash off to Paris, interludes of an apartment on Fifth
Avenue—but always a place to be going from.

Osa Johnson, *I Married Adventure*, 1940

The Open Road. The great home of the soul is the Open
Road. Not Heaven, not paradise. Not "above." Not even
"within." It is a wayfarer down the road.

**D. H. Lawrence (1885–1930) English novelist,
poet, "Whitman"**

Oh I found so many beautiful things
As I roamed the wide world o'er,
And they sang a song that soars and sings
Around me evermore.

Anonymous

129

FLINGING MONKEYS AT THE COCONUTS

I been a wanderin'
Early and late.
New York City
To the Golden Gate
An' it looks like
I'm never gonna cease my
Wanderin'.

**Carl Sandburg (1878-1967) American poet,
folk-music lyrics recalled on his death,
July 22, 1967**

The biggest discovery of all was about myself: On the
back roads of America, I felt at home at last. I knew I
wanted to spend the rest of my life out there.

**Charles Kuralt (b. 1934) American journalist,
A Life on the Road, 1990**

. . . there is certainly a part of me that would like to
travel again. The vast world is forever calling.

**Nick Danziger (b. 1958) English-American artist,
author, *Danziger's Travels*, 1987**

Index of authors

INDEX OF AUTHORS

"Take my word for it!"

About the author

Intrepid world traveler and quotations anthologist, TREVOR KENNER CRALLE (rhymes with "trolley"), has a degree in cultural geography from the University of California, Berkeley. Born in 1961 and named for British actor Trevor Howard, Trevor began to wander at an early age and soon developed an incurable longing to go to the ends of the earth. His peregrinations have taken him to over forty countries throughout Europe, the Caribbean, Latin America, South Pacific and Southeast Asia.

A native California surfer, Trevor is also a surf linguist and surf slang lexicographer, known to many as "The Webster of the Waves" for his book, *The Surfin'ary: A Dictionary of Surfing Terms and Surfspeak* (Ten Speed Press 1991), which received a gnarlatious wave of international media attention.

As a roving ambassador for the Rainforest Action Network headquartered in San Francisco, he has lectured extensively around the Bay Area and led several high school expeditions through Costa Rica's rainforests. Trevor has worked for the California Coastal Commission as one of the principal writers and a contributing photographer to the *California Coastal Resource Guide* and best-selling companion *California Coastal Access Guide*. He is currently working on a book of his own travel essays. Trevor enjoys hanging out in tropical places where thirst-quenching green coconuts are readily available.

photo by Ellen Nachtigall

I'm the ramblin' son with the nervous feet
That never was made for a steady beat.
I had many a job for a little while;
I've been on the bum, and I've lived in style,
But there was the road windin' mile after mile,
And nothing to do but go.

**H. H. Knibbs (1874–1945) poet,
"Nothing to Do But Go"**